342
LAW

Lawson, Don

The changing face of
the Constitution

DATE			
FE 06 '87			
DEC 2 0 '91			

6 90

The Changing Face of the Constitution

The Changing Face of the Constitution

Prohibition, Universal Suffrage and Women's Rights, Civil Rights, and Religious Freedom

Don Lawson

FRANKLIN WATTS
NEW YORK | LONDON | 1979

Library of Congress Cataloging in Publication Data

Lawson, Don.
　The changing face of the Constitution.

　Bibliography: p.
　Includes index.
　SUMMARY: A history of the American Constitution focusing on certain key Supreme Court decisions that have made changes in the original document.
　　1. United States—Constitutional law—Juvenile
literature. [1. United States—Constitutional law]
I. Title.
KF4550.Z9L39　　　342'.73'029　　　78–11570
ISBN 0–531–02923–9

Contents

The Changing Face of the Constitution

Creating a Living Constitution

The United States has the oldest written constitution in the world. It was drafted by the Founding Fathers in 1787. The following year it was ratified by the required number of states—nine out of the original thirteen—and it went into effect in 1789. The other states ratified it later.

Almost immediately the American Constitution was recognized as a model for democratic nations everywhere. Many statesmen regarded it as a work of genius. William Gladstone, the great British statesman, described it as "the most wonderful work ever struck off by the brain of man." Today it is as vital and sound a document as it was when it was written more than two centuries ago.

How has the United States Constitution stood the test of time so well?

3

Mainly because of its flexibility. It is actually a short document for a work of its kind; it is only about four thousand words. Many of America's fifty states have constitutions that are much longer. But the very brevity of the federal Constitution has been one of the keys to its success.

It was the genius of the Founding Fathers that made it possible for them to create a "living constitution." They knew they were preparing a document that was to be the supreme law of the land. But they were also wise enough to know that it would be a mistake to try to "nail everything down" for all time. The Constitution had to be able to respond to the challenges of future generations or it would die. James Madison perhaps expressed it best when he said: "In framing a system which we wish to last for ages, we should not lose sight of the changes which ages will produce."

The Founding Fathers had no way of knowing, of course, that their small nation of between 3 and 4 million people—most of whom were farmers—would one day grow into an industrial giant of some 220 million people. But they did know that the United States would grow and change, and they provided the means for the Constitution to respond to the challenge of this growth and change. The two most important means provided were *amendment* and *interpretation*.

4

Constitutional Amendments

Amendments to the Constitution are provided for in the Constitution itself in Article V. Amendments may be proposed by a two-thirds vote of each house of Congress. They may also be proposed by national conventions called by Congress. The amendments must then be ratified by the legislatures of three-fourths of the states or by conventions in three-fourths of the states.

The passage of amendments is a slow, orderly, and even tiresome process. This prevents petty tampering with the basic law of the land. Consequently, there have been relatively few amendments to the Constitution. The first ten—called the Bill of Rights—were added in 1791. They dealt mainly with the protection of individual liberties. Actually, they might easily have been a part of the original Constitution. Several states said they would only ratify the Constitution if these amendments guaranteeing personal liberty and private property rights were added. The Founding Fathers agreed.

Since 1791 only sixteen amendments have been added, making a total of twenty-six in all. Most of these last sixteen have been added since the Civil War. All, of course, have been of great importance, not only in reshaping the Constitution itself but also in reshaping American society. They have dealt with broad moral, ethical, and spiritual challenges to the Constitution, that is, slavery, religious freedom, the rights and duties of citizens, and so on. They have also dealt with more worldly matters such as the method of presidential elec-

5

tion and succession, voting rights, and the regulation of commerce and industry.

Constitutional Interpretation

When asked exactly what the job of the Supreme Court was, Supreme Court Chief Justice Charles Evans Hughes—one of the nation's great judges and an equally great baseball fan—liked to tell the story of his favorite hometown baseball umpire. Overhearing some fans one day discussing the importance of the baseball rule book in making decisions on certain plays, the grizzled old umpire commented: "A play ain't *nothin'* until *I* say what it is!" And that, explained Chief Justice Hughes, is the role of the Supreme Court. "We are under a Constitution, but the Constitution is what the judges say it is."

The Founding Fathers probably did not intend the Supreme Court to assume the power that it has today. They expected it to play a relatively minor role in interpreting the Constitution and making any questions on points of law clear. However, providing for a Supreme Court was perhaps one of the wisest decisions the framers of the Constitution made. The Supreme Court has responded strongly to the challenges of the nation's growth and change, and its decisions have kept the Constitution more up to date than all of the twenty-six amendments put together.

6

The Supreme Court is provided for in the Constitution in Article III, which begins simply: "The judicial power of the United States shall be vested in one Supreme Court. . . ." From that simple sentence has grown the most powerful court in the world.

"Equal Justice Under Law"

The Supreme Court had humble beginnings. For many years it was housed in several small, dark rooms in the basement of the nation's Capitol. These quarters were so inadequate that the justices had to put on their robes in public. Later, the Court occupied what had formerly been the Senate chambers. Since 1935, however, it has had its own handsome marble building across a plaza east of the Capitol. The tall twin rows of Corinthian columns at the front of the building make it look like a Greek temple. Over the entrance the following words are carved: "Equal Justice Under Law." The justices spend their lives living up to this motto.

The Supreme Court is made up of a chief justice and eight associate justices. All are appointed by the president and must be confirmed by the Senate. Their number varied between six and ten until after the Civil War. Then, today's total of nine was permanently established. Justices may remain in office for life, subject only to good behavior. A justice's conduct is a matter which may be determined by the Senate.

Only one justice has ever been impeached. This was Samuel Chase, a signer of the Declaration of Independence. In 1804, Chase, a political opponent of Thomas Jefferson, was accused of making seditious statements about the Jefferson administration. The Senate, however, failed to convict Chase. His acquittal helped establish the independence of the Supreme Court.

"The Great Chief Justice"

The man who undoubtedly did the most to establish the Supreme Court's authority in interpreting the supreme law of the land and in declaring acts of Congress constitutional or unconstitutional was Chief Justice John Marshall. Marshall is still called "The Great Chief Justice" by our nation's lawyers.

Born in a log cabin in Virginia in 1755, Marshall fought as a boy in several of the most important battles of the American Revolution. All of his life he remained an ardent patriot. "I went into the Revolution a Virginian," he said, "and came out an American."

After the war Marshall studied law. As a lawyer he was active in getting Virginia to adopt the new U.S. Constitution. President John Adams appointed Marshall fourth chief justice of the Supreme Court in 1801. He served in that role until his death thirty-four years later.

8

When Marshall took over as chief justice, the Court's reputation was so bad that few men wanted to serve on it. Within a matter of a very few years Marshall had transformed the Court into a strong and vigorous third branch of the government. It became equal in every way to the executive and legislative branches.

Marshall brought about this transformation by leading the Court in rendering decisions that greatly strengthened the federal government. In a series of vital cases, Marshall almost single-handedly established the power of the Supreme Court to declare laws unconstitutional. The Marshall Court also made it clear that federal power must prevail over state power if the two were ever in conflict. If these points had not been firmly established early in the history of the Constitution, that document would have become weak and useless. Marshall's interpretations not only strengthened the Constitution but they also strengthened the country. They enabled the United States to take its place among the great democracies of the world. In addition, many of Marshall's decisions are as valid and alive and meaningful to the challenge of today's world as they were when they were first made.

There have been many great chief justices and associate justices since John Marshall's day. All, of course, have not been great, since justices, like everybody else, are human beings and subject to frailty and error. They have all, however, rendered decisions to the best of their considerable abilities.

This has also been true of the members of Congress who have passed, or failed to pass, certain amend-

9

ments to the Constitution. Certainly not all of the amendments that have been passed have been 100 percent right. Moreover, at least one was so unpopular that it eventually was repealed. This was the Eighteenth or Prohibition Amendment.

Prohibition

The only amendment to the United States Constitution that has ever been repealed was the Eighteenth
or Prohibition Amendment. It prohibited the manufacture and sale of alcoholic or intoxicating beverages
within the United States. It was repealed by the
Twenty-first Amendment.

Prohibition presented one of the most important
challenges not only to the U.S. Constitution but also to
American society. The country still feels its effects today from the grip that organized crime has managed to
maintain on such things as the traffic in drugs, illegal
gambling, and other forms of vice. Many of these criminals are the direct descendants of the gangsters who got
their start during the wild and lawless Prohibition era.

The Prohibition Amendment was actually the result of a widespread desire to improve society. It grew

11

out of the crusading spirit for all kinds of moral and social reform with which people were filled during World War I. Although Prohibition had nothing to do with the war itself, it resulted from an important part of the psychology of the war which emphasized the spirit of sacrifice. Americans went into the conflict with a crusading desire to make the world in general and their country in particular a better place in which to live. The end of the war brought disillusionment and bitterness when people saw that the four years of fighting had brought great destruction and death. Nonetheless, the crusading spirit for reform remained. Prohibition was one of the outcomes. A second result was the passage of the Nineteenth Amendment, which gave women the right to vote.

Beginnings of the Temperance Movement

The prohibition or temperance movement in America began well before the Civil War, but its progress was slow until World War I. By 1900, only five states had passed statewide prohibition acts, and several others had what was called "local option." This meant town governments could declare their towns were "dry." However, by the middle of World War I, some thirty states had prohibition of some kind. The success of the prohibition movement up to this point was largely due to the work of the Women's Christian Temperance

12

Union (WCTU), founded by Frances Willard, and the Anti-Saloon League, which was led by the militant Wayne B. Wheeler. The temperance movement was also aided by the women's rights movement. Women forcefully declared that they wanted their hard-working husbands to bring home their pay envelopes to support their families rather than to spend their pay in local saloons.

In 1917, the year America entered World War I, Congress passed a statute prohibiting the public sale of liquor. This was a wartime food-control measure aimed at saving grain for food rather than using it to make alcohol. That same year Congress voted to submit the Eighteenth Amendment to the states. It was ratified by the states with relative speed and became a part of the Constitution on January 29, 1919. It went into effect on January 16, 1920. A law providing for federal enforcement of the Prohibition Amendment was passed on October 28, 1919. This law was called the Volstead Act after its sponsor, Congressman Andrew Volstead of Minnesota. Actually the law was written by Anti-Saloon League leader, Wayne Wheeler. It was vetoed by President Woodrow Wilson, but Congress quickly passed it over his veto.

Almost immediately the Eighteenth Amendment was attacked as being unconstitutional. This was interesting because it marked the first time in history that a constitutional amendment, which was technically a part of the Constitution itself, was attacked as unconstitutional. The Supreme Court, however, quickly disposed of this possibility by declaring in 1920 that the

13

Eighteenth Amendment was a valid part of the Constitution and thus automatically a legitimate law of the land.

But the fight over Prohibition, especially its enforcement, had just begun.

Satisfying the Public Thirst

When the Prohibition Amendment was passed, almost everyone simply assumed it would be accepted. This was a serious misjudgment. In addition, one of the major mistakes made by the sponsors of the amendment was to claim too many benefits would result from its passage. Pamphlets issued by the Anti-Saloon League claimed that alcohol was responsible for poverty, disease, crime, and even insanity. Prohibition, the pamphlets said, would make it possible for the country to eliminate jails, asylums, and senior citizens homes.

When the Eighteenth Amendment was passed and none of these benefits resulted, people quickly became disillusioned. Furthermore, with the war over and wartime restraints no longer in effect, people seemed ready for peacetime freedom of action. It quickly became clear that the American people had absolutely no intention of doing without alcoholic beverages even if it meant breaking the law to get them. To satisfy this thirst a whole new industry sprang up. It was called "bootlegging." This term came from the early practice of smug-

14

glers hiding contraband in the tops of their boots. Eventually bootlegging came to mean the entire operation of making, transporting, and selling alcoholic beverages.

Almost overnight a major liquor and beer smuggling business began. Despite the fact that thousands of arrests were made under the Volstead Prohibition Enforcement Act, bootlegging increased. Within ten years federal agents had made more than half a million arrests and obtained several hundred thousand convictions. Nevertheless, the illegal beer and liquor trade continued to grow. It grew because there was big money, millions and millions of dollars, in it.

Bootleggers, Rum Runners, and Moonshiners

Many bootleggers smuggled their wares across the Canadian and Mexican borders. Others smuggled liquor in by boat. Liquor-laden freighters sailed from such places as Cuba and the Bahama Islands where there was no prohibition. These freighters would anchor offshore, beyond the twelve-mile limit, where they could be safely out of the reach of the United States Coast Guard and other enforcement agencies. The liquor then would be transferred to small, high-powered boats. These transfer boats would be docked and unloaded at isolated places along the Eastern seaboard. Bootleggers thus engaged were called "rum runners."

Once the liquor was ashore, it was transferred to

trucks and hauled inland for illegal sale. Along the way, rival bootleggers might "hijack" the trucks and steal the liquor. Warfare between criminal gangs was often the result. One of the things that made this type of smuggling possible was the relatively recent development of the automobile and the truck. Without them bootlegging could never have become such a big business.

Another thing that made the smuggling of liquor so easy was the enormous length of America's borders—some nineteen thousand miles of land borders and coastline. It was estimated that if all of the nation's Prohibition enforcement agents were stationed along the land and sea borders, each agent would have to patrol an area of twelve miles. (This would be like trying to station guards along today's Alaskan oil pipeline to protect it against saboteurs.) Furthermore, these agents were poorly paid—they earned between two thousand and three thousand dollars a year—so it was never too difficult for bootleggers to bribe one of them to look the other way when a shipment of alcohol was entering the United States.

There were also many illegal stills for the manufacture of alcohol hidden away in remote areas of the Appalachian Mountains. Alcohol from these stills was called "moonshine" (because the stills were supposedly operated at night, or by "the light of the moon"), and the men who operated them were called "moonshiners." Illegal stills and breweries were also operated in huge apparently abandoned warehouses in all of the major cities. These stills and breweries were usually run by

16

organized criminal gangs who controlled the illegal manufacture and sale of liquor and beer in their particular cities. Warfare often broke out between these gangs for continued control of the multimillion-dollar bootleg liquor business. Gangs also owned many nightclubs and "speakeasies"—illicit drinking establishments —so they were certain of outlets for their liquor and beer.

Industrial alcohol and alcohol for medicinal purposes could legally be manufactured. Much of this also found its way into the bootleg liquor trade. Druggists, for example, could legally sell alcohol for medicinal purposes, and as a result drugstores became common outlets for bootleg liquor. Unfortunately, some methyl or wood alcohol intended for use as a fuel or as automobile antifreeze was occasionally sold for drinking purposes. Many cases of blindness and death were the result. In 1925 alone, the national death toll from drinking poisoned liquor was more than four thousand persons.

People who preferred not to patronize bootleggers and speakeasies but still wanted to drink alcoholic beverages often made their own "homebrew" or "bathtub gin." Grocery stores sold malt and hops for the manufacture of home-brewed beer. Also, grape juice with yeast added to it could be allowed to ferment and thus produce a passable wine. Many people also bought grape presses and squeezed their own grapes for homemade wine. Bathtub gin was nothing more than grain alcohol (purchased illegally, perhaps from the corner druggist) with juniper berry flavoring added.

17

The Big Business of Bootlegging

The production of alcoholic drinks in the home was small business as compared with the bootlegging industry. This industry led to the establishment of a major criminal class and links between the police and organized crime. In many cities, these associations have never been broken. In Chicago alone, for example, there were literally hundreds of gangland murders during the Prohibition era that never were solved. Former Chicago Police Chief Charles C. Fitzmorris admitted that 60 percent of his police were in the bootlegging business.

One of the high points in this criminal carnival was reached in 1929 when the bootlegging-fed feud between Al Capone's gang and George "Bugs" Moran's gang resulted in the St. Valentine's Day Massacre. In this case, seven members of the Moran gang were machine-gunned to death by several Capone hoodlums. Capone's men dressed as policemen, "raided" the North Side garage where the victims were preparing to buy a truckload of hijacked alcohol, and murdered their rivals.

No one was ever punished for this mass assassination. Capone himself was virtually in control of Chicago and seemingly immune to prosecution. However, a number of years later he was convicted of federal income tax evasion and was sent to prison. Nevertheless, the descendants of his criminal organization still infest the city today, and much the same dark story can be told about New York, Los Angeles, Detroit, Toledo, and many other American cities.

18

The Rise of Al Capone

Al Capone—or Al Brown, as he was originally known—got his start when he was invited to Chicago from New York to act as assistant and bodyguard to South Side hoodlum Johnny Torrio. Torrio was business manager for Big Jim Colosimo, a millionaire bootlegger who owned a cafe bearing his name on Chicago's South Wabash Avenue. It was in this restaurant that Big Jim Colosimo was gunned down one afternoon. Torrio and Capone were suspected of having Colosimo killed so they could take over his flourishing bootlegging business. Nothing was ever proved against Torrio and Capone, but they did indeed inherit Colosimo's liquor and beer operation.

Torrio and Capone immediately began to expand their bootlegging empire. They opened numerous cafes, nightclubs, and speakeasies throughout the South Side of Chicago and even in the suburbs. In order to supply the Chicago outlets, whole fleets of trucks brought bonded liquor down from the Canadian border, and moonshine was brought in from Ohio and Kentucky. The brewing of beer for local distribution was done right in Chicago and nearby suburbs. Police protection was essential to this operation, and it was obtained simply by putting scores of Chicago police on the Torrio-Capone payroll.

The Death of Dion O'Banion

Chicago's North Side bootlegging empire was controlled by a florist named Dion O'Banion. Gang warfare frequently broke out between the North and South Side hoodlums. When it did, Capone mobilized his one-hundred-man army that protected the Torrio-Capone interests. Eventually this warfare resulted in O'Banion's untimely demise, following an attempt by O'Banion's gang to invade the Torrio-Capone South Side territory.

On November 10, 1924, several well-dressed men walked into O'Banion's flower shop on North State Street, apparently to buy flower arrangements for a recently departed hoodlum friend. One man shook O'Banion's hand in a friendly fashion while the two other men took out guns and shot him to death. Torrio and Capone were among the two most prominent mourners at O'Banion's funeral. It was one of the most lavish in Chicago's history, and there were more than fifty thousand dollars worth of memorial flowers there. Among the wreaths there was a huge basket of roses with a card from Al Capone. The flowers had been ordered from the late Dion O'Banion's shop.

O'Banion's North Side successor as gang boss was Hymie Weiss. His aide was Bugs Moran. Weiss and Moran vowed to revenge O'Banion's death, and soon the bodies of assassinated hoodlums began to litter Chicago's streets. During one five-year period there were more than five hundred such slayings.

In late January 1925 Torrio was almost killed when

he was ambushed by Weiss-Moran gunmen outside of his South Side apartment building. Although Torrio gradually recovered from his half a dozen wounds, he did not forget the pain they had caused him. The pain was made even greater because the bullets that wounded him had been rubbed with garlic. Torrio was also in growing fear for his life if he continued in the bootlegging business. He was now a multimillionaire, and with his wife's encouragement, he decided to enjoy some of the money before it was too late.

Calling Al Capone to his side, Torrio turned the South Side bootlegging business over to him and sailed for Europe.

Capone Takes Over Chicago

Capone now proceeded to take over the whole of Chicago's gangland empire. His method was one of total violence combined with political alliances with the police forces and civil administrations of Chicago and its suburbs. Capone had his headquarters in the suburb of Cicero. In Cicero's Hawthorne Hotel Capone lived like a feudal baron in a heavily guarded castle. When he ventured outside his castle he traveled in a heavily armored car. Accompanying this mobile fortress were patrol cars filled with his henchmen to protect Capone from attack.

By way of violence, Capone first had Hymie Weiss

21

gunned down in front of the former O'Banion flower shop. Numerous Capone-mob assassinations followed, culminating in the brutal St. Valentine's Day Massacre. Increasing his army to more than one thousand gunmen, Capone soon had control of the South and West sides of Chicago as well as many of the other suburbs besides Cicero. In several of the suburbs he controlled politicians and elections right along with the bootlegging business. His income was estimated at $100 million a year. The mayor of Cicero had been personally selected and installed in office by Capone, and even the Chicago Mayor William Hale "Big Bill" Thompson was deeply in Capone's debt. An open alliance between Thompson's administration and the mob was never proved. However, Thompson did accept hundreds of thousands of dollars from the Capone organization in "campaign contributions" in exchange for Thompson's pledge to instruct city police to keep "hands off" the bootlegging business. Many citizens believed that Thompson was mayor in name only, and that it was Capone who was truly running the city.

Growth of Gangland Rackets

Prohibition also spawned another major criminal enterprise. This was the "protection racket" from which the country still suffers today. Here again Capone led the way. Three-quarters of Capone's estimated $100 million annual income came from beer and liquor sales. The rest came from gambling, prostitution, nightclubs, and the rackets.

Rackets and racketeering simply meant blackmailing or extorting money from businessmen in return for "protection." The protection consisted mainly of *not* destroying a man's business enterprise if he agreed to pay the blackmail or protection money. If he refused to pay, his business was destroyed.

Capone did not invent the rackets. They were started by early labor union organizers who used bombs to destroy anti-union factories and to intimidate their owners. Some of these labor leaders—by no means all—also hired thugs. They used these gunmen to protect themselves from retaliation by businessmen whose enterprises were attacked and also from other labor organizers vying for union control. Since many of these thugs and gunmen came from Capone's gangs, the next logical step was for Capone to enter the protection racket himself. This he did, with certain refinements, and the rackets swiftly spread from coast to coast.

In some cases the gangsters simply took over labor unions and used them for their own criminal purposes. In others they pretended to establish unions. However, these fronts were merely cover-ups for extortion and blackmail rings. In all cases businessmen either agreed to pay the protection money or their means of making a living were destroyed. They too might be personally injured or killed. If the blackmailed businessman com-

23

plained to the authorities, this seldom did any good because the authorities were either on the mob payrolls or afraid to act.

In Chicago alone during the 1920s there were about one hundred different rackets, and they cost the public—who paid the final bill—millions of dollars a year. They included the cleaners and dyers, garage, and window-washing rackets as well as those that preyed on restaurant owners, laundry owners, clothing store proprietors and others. Each owner paid regular protection dues to the Capone mobsters or suffered the results. If businessmen did not cooperate, their establishments were often bombed. A cleaners' and dyers', a laundry, or a clothing store might be invaded by acid-throwing hoodlums and all clothing in them destroyed. Or, all of the cars in a garage or apartments in a building might have their windows smashed. The results were inevitable. Proprietors either finally paid for protection, or they went out of business.

Downfall of Capone

Eventually it was public opinion as much as anything else that brought about Al Capone's downfall. Gradually the Chicago citizenry became sick and tired of living in a completely crime-ridden city. The St. Valentine's Day Massacre had been simply too much for law-abiding people to tolerate. Their reaction against

Mayor Thompson's regime began to be expressed at the polls and in the newspapers. In local elections, anti-Thompson candidates began to be elected. The newspapers began to blast the city administration's links with the underworld. Simultaneously, Capone himself began to get into trouble.

While on a visit to Philadelphia, Capone was arrested for carrying a concealed weapon and sentenced to a year in jail. When he got out of jail after serving ten months of his sentence, he returned to Chicago. However, he found that the city's atmosphere had changed. Almost immediately he was picked up by police and put in jail for vagrancy. This had been happening to his henchmen for months. When they complained at this kind of harassment, they were simply thrown back into jail on new vagrancy charges.

In addition, strong new efforts were being made to enforce the Volstead Act. In May 1930, Prohibition enforcement was transferred from the U.S. Treasury Department to the Department of Justice. Thus, for a time at least, the mass arrest and conviction of Volstead Act violators slowed down the flow of bootleg beer and liquor. In Chicago, a squad of federal agents headed by a scrupulously honest young man named Elliot Ness earned the nickname, "The Untouchables." They were dedicated to destroying the Capone mob's bootlegging business, and they could not be bribed. Capone himself learned that Ness and his men really were untouchable when the mob leader offered them a percentage of the profits from his beer business only to have them respond by wrecking several Capone breweries.

25

Other federal agents, these from the Internal Revenue Service, also began to taken an active interest in Capone's business affairs. Capone's gross profit had been an estimated $400 million since he had taken charge, but the mob chief had never filed an income tax return. At the urging of President Herbert Hoover, Treasury Secretary Andrew Mellon instructed IRS agents to take action against Capone and his followers for income tax evasion.

Capone's brother, Ralph, was the first to go to jail early in 1930. While the IRS was hot on Al Capone's trail, a Chicago *Tribune* reporter named Alfred "Jake" Lingle was shot to death by gangsters. It was believed that Lingle had gangland connections and had information about Capone's sources of income. Rumor had it that Lingle was about to turn this information over to IRS agents. It was believed that he was gunned down to prevent him from talking. This did not, however, slow down the IRS investigation of Capone.

In the spring of 1931 Capone was indicted for income tax evasion. In October he was convicted and sentenced to a lengthy term in a federal penitentiary. That November, a reform mayoral candidate, Anton J. Cermak, defeated Big Bill Thompson's bid for reelection as mayor of Chicago. Thompson did not endear himself to the ethnic electorate when during the course of the campaign he cast slurs on Cermak's Bohemian ancestry.

Cermak began an immediate series of civic reforms. These reforms were vigorous and widespread. However, he was assassinated by Giuseppe Zangara while accom-

26

panying President-elect Franklin D. Roosevelt on a public appearance trip to Miami, Florida, in 1933. The crazed gunman was apparently trying to kill Roosevelt and hit Cermak by mistake. Shortly after he was shot, Cermak said to Roosevelt: "I'm glad it was me instead of you."

Prohibition Repealed Under FDR

It was during the first term in office of Franklin D. Roosevelt (or FDR as he was popularly known), that the Prohibition Amendment was finally repealed. Actually, even though FDR was a confirmed "wet," or believer in repeal, he was not principally responsible for repeal. This probably would have happened no matter who was elected to the presidency.

The public, which had never really been strongly in favor of "The Noble Experiment," as President Herbert Hoover called the Eighteenth Amendment, was now downright disgusted with it. Three successive Republican Presidents, Warren Harding, Calvin Coolidge, and Herbert Hoover had made only pious-sounding statements about enforcing the Volstead Act even though Coolidge and Hoover were both considered "drys." This was mainly because Coolidge and Hoover were political conservatives who thought the best kind of government was the least amount of government control. Consequently, they did not think the government should tell people what they should or should not drink. Harding was a confirmed drinker in and out of the White House. At weekly White House poker parties Harding's wife, Florence, served her husband and his card-playing cronies bourbon highballs.

Nevertheless, all three of these presidents did at least go through the motions of making federal law enforcement agencies do their job since the Eighteenth Amendment was indeed a part of the law of the land. Hoover went so far as to promise the "drys" that he would have a government commission study the Prohibition problem if he were elected to the presidency in 1928. This pledge helped him defeat the Democratic candidate, Governor Alfred E. Smith of New York, a confirmed "wet." Two months after taking office Hoover appointed an eleven-man commission under the chairmanship of George W. Wickersham of New York.

The Wickersham Report

The Wickersham Committee was more than thorough in its work. It took them almost two years to complete their report, which was handed to Hoover in January, 1931. The report proved to be confusing to say the least. The committee as a whole agreed that Prohibition, while it seemed impossible to enforce, should be continued. However, each of the eleven members turned in separate reports and of these, five favored

Prohibition without change, four favored modification of the amendment with such changes as allowing the individual states to decide whether they wanted to be "wet" or "dry," and two members were flatly in favor of the amendment's repeal. ("Wets" favored repeal. "Drys" did not.) What the Wickersham report clearly said was that Prohibition simply was not working—a fact which everybody already knew.

The man who was most pleased with the confusion caused by the Wickersham report was FDR. He was then governor of New York and planned to run as the Democratic nominee for president against the incumbent, Herbert Hoover, in 1932. FDR favored repeal and he sensed he had the country behind him in this as well as in other matters. Hoover, on the other hand, had aligned himself with the "drys" by creating the Wickersham Committee, and FDR knew this alignment would help defeat Hoover. FDR was right.

FDR's First Hundred Days

In 1932, the United States was suffering from the worst economic depression in its history. Hoover believed the country could work its way out of the depression if the government kept "hands off" the economy. FDR believed the situation called for radical government action—what he called, "A New Deal for the American people."

FDR was elected in a landslide vote by a public that wanted dramatic change. FDR began to provide this change as soon as he took office. During FDR's "First Hundred Days," as historians call the beginning of his New Deal administration, more legislation was proposed and passed by the Congress in that short time than ever before in history.

One of the first things FDR did, on March 13, 1933, was to ask Congress to change the Volstead Act to allow the manufacture and sale of light wines and 3.2 beer (beer that contained no more than 3.2 percent of alcohol). This the Congress readily agreed to because even before FDR was inaugurated Congress had voted to submit the Twenty-first Amendment repealing Prohibition to the states for ratification.

In record time, just as they had ratified the Prohibition Amendment, the states ratified the repeal amendment. Utah was the last of the necessary thirty-six states to do so. Utah's ratification came on December 5, 1933. "The Noble Experiment" had ended.

Why "The Noble Experiment" Failed

If the Prohibition Amendment taught no other lesson, it taught a clear and simple one about life in a democracy: if the majority of the people do not believe in a law, that law simply cannot be enforced. It was true, of course, that before the Eighteenth Amendment was passed people in general were apparently in favor of it. As a result, Prohibition became a law almost casually. But when the test of total abstinence really came, the majority of the people simply would not accept it.

A similar situation arose in the 1970s when efforts were made to enforce a uniform maximum vehicle speed limit of 55 miles per hour on the nation's highways. For a time the driving public went along with it. But soon it was being ignored on most major highways despite the countless thousands of arrests that were made and despite the fact that reduced highway speeds saved not only gasoline but also lives.

The lesson proved a costly one in the case of Prohibition. The U.S. Justice Department estimated that the federal government alone had spent about $130 million in a futile attempt to enforce it. Almost one hundred federal agents and almost two hundred civilians had been killed in the process of enforcement, and some half a million people had gone to jail for breaking Prohibition laws. Far more serious, however, was the fact that literally millions of other people—ordinary citizens—had broken the law without being caught. This taught them a certain disrespect for the laws of the land. Further, a major hold on American society had been gained by criminal gangs. This hold was apparently unbreakable, because it was never broken even after the repeal of Prohibition.

Women's Role in the Prohibition Era

One of the major changes brought about by Prohibition was the enormous increase in public drinking on the part of women. This was brought about essentially by two things. The first was women's growing legal and social freedom or emancipation and the growing acceptance of their equality with men. Part of this was due to their obtaining the right to vote with the passage of the Nineteenth Amendment on August 26, 1920. The second thing was the establishment of the Prohibition era speakeasy.

Before Prohibition, respectable women were almost never seen at the bar of the old-fashioned saloon. When Prohibition closed the saloons, the illicit speakeasies took their place, and here women were generally accepted. Public drinking, smoking cigarettes, cutting or "bobbing" one's hair, knee-length skirts, and growing sexual freedom were all expressions of women's emancipation in the 1920s. When Prohibition was repealed and public drinking establishments again became legal (called "taverns" now rather than "saloons," at FDR's request), women took their place at the bar right alongside men.

Interestingly, one of the most successful of all of the Volstead Act enforcement officials had been a woman. This was a young West Coast lawyer named Mabel Walker Willebrandt. She was appointed assistant attorney general in charge of Prohibition enforcement by President Warren Harding in 1921. Harding made this appointment mainly to follow a precedent set by his predecessor, Woodrow Wilson, who had appointed Annette Abbot Adams of San Francisco as the first woman assistant attorney general in the nation's history.

Mrs. Willebrandt, who divorced her husband when marriage interfered with her career, had devoted her early law career to defending young Los Angeles women. Her clients included abandoned mothers, prostitutes, and other unfortunates. Although she was a moderate drinker herself, she completely gave up drinking when she took the Prohibition enforcement job with the U.S. government. She was a totally dedicated lawyer, as she continued to prove in her role as assistant attorney general. Despite a considerable amount of opposition simply because she was a woman, Mrs. Willebrandt was successful in smashing major bootlegging operations in Savannah, Georgia, and Cincinnati, Ohio. She was also successful in prosecuting their leaders. In addition, she appeared before the Supreme Court to successfully defend convictions she had obtained against Volstead Act violators when these convictions were claimed to be unconstitutional.

However, despite her successful record, Mabel Walker Willebrandt resigned as assistant attorney general after eight long years of frustrating work to enforce what was basically an unenforceable law. When she left office, she spoke kindly of then President Herbert Hoover's continuing efforts to "dam the alcoholic flood." However, then she took a job in California as an attorney for Fruit Industries, Inc. Fruit Industries, Inc., had just received several millions of dollars in loans from the federal government. One of the things it was going to do with this money was to market a new grape juice product called Vine-Glo.

Although Vine-Glo was nonalcoholic, it came in various wine flavors, that is, sherry, port, muscatel, and so on. If sugar were added to it and the mixture were allowed to ferment for a few weeks, genuine wine with a potent alcoholic content would result. The product, obviously aimed at customers who wanted to evade the Prohibition law, was an overnight success throughout the forty-eight states. Mabel Walker Willebrandt's story, with its ironic ending, was the fitting finale to the Prohibition era.

Universal Suffrage and Women's Rights

American democracy has often been compared with the democracy of ancient Greece. This comparison is a good one because both democracies fostered a spirit of individual freedom and human liberty that has seldom been matched in world history. However, American democracy and Greek democracy had their bad points too. In ancient Athens, for example, neither slaves nor women could vote. Exactly the same situation held true in the United States until relatively recent times.

Universal suffrage means the right or privilege of all of a nation's adult citizens, male and female, to vote in the nation's political matters. This issue has been a challenge to the United States Constitution from the days of the Founding Fathers right up until the present. However, as Supreme Court Chief Justice Earl Warren

35

observed in 1964: "History has seen a continuing expansion of the scope of the right of suffrage in this country."

Proof of Chief Justice Warren's observation can be seen in the following accomplishments: the Fifteenth Amendment to the United States Constitution, adopted in 1870, gave blacks the right to vote. (The Thirteenth Amendment had abolished slavery, but it did not give blacks the vote.) The Nineteenth Amendment, adopted in 1920, extended suffrage to women. The Twenty-fourth Amendment, adopted in 1964, barred poll or head taxes—that is, a tax paid by each person who votes. Such taxes, which were intended to prevent poor people, especially blacks, from voting, were also abolished in state elections by a Supreme Court ruling in 1966. The Voting Rights Act, passed in 1965 and later extended, suspended state literacy and other voting qualification tests. The Twenty-sixth Amendment, adopted in 1971, set the voting age for all federal, state, and local elections at eighteen.

Subject to the above restrictions, the Constitution guarantees each state and the District of Columbia the right to decide the qualifications of their voters. Those qualified to vote in state elections are also eligible to vote in national elections. The right of the states to decide who can vote goes back to colonial times.

Voting in the Colonies

In America's original thirteen colonies only men could vote. However, the privilege did not extend to all men. Usually a man had to own a certain amount of property—perhaps fifty acres—or property that earned him a certain amount of income. This was a system that was carried over from England where most of the colonists came from. The system was called the "forty shilling freehold." This meant that in order to vote a man had to own property that earned him forty shillings a year—approximately seven hundred fifty dollars in today's money.

Sometimes there were religious qualifications for voting. In Massachusetts, for example, as late as 1664 a man had to belong to the Congregational church to qualify as a voter. At about the time of the American Revolution several colonies disqualified all non-Protestants from voting. All of the Southern colonies barred blacks from voting, and all of the colonies always barred Indians.

After the Revolution most of the original colonies adopted new constitutions, and new states adopted constitutions when they were admitted to the Union. All of these documents contained regulations about who qualified to vote. They contained property-ownership as well as other voting restrictions. Also, the framers of the state constitutions made the mistake that the Founding Fathers did not make when they wrote the U.S. Constitution: the former tried to foresee every possible

37

future problem and nail down the solution. The next century was spent in trying to simplify these state constitutions. In doing so, one great step forward was made: more and more voting restrictions were removed.

Voting in the Early United States

New Hampshire was the first to adopt universal white male suffrage, in 1784. Shortly afterward Delaware allowed all adult white taxpayers to vote, and Kentucky declared that all free males over twenty-one could vote. Vermont limited its balloting only to the "freemen of each town." So it went as new states joined the Union and proceeded to modify their constitutions. Universal suffrage for all adult men and women was far from achieved, but progress was being made. The greatest strides forward were not made, however, until the nineteenth century.

As is the case with most human progress, the greater the advancements that were made toward universal suffrage the more difficult they were to achieve.

In the first half of the nineteenth century Maryland, Massachusetts, New York, and Rhode Island all abolished property qualifications for voting—but only for adult white males. "Persons of color" were not included. Even universal suffrage for white men was bitterly contested. In Rhode Island the controversy almost caused a war in the 1840s.

38

The Dorr Rebellion, as the Rhode Island struggle was called, began when non-property-owning men demanded that they be allowed to vote. The revolt, led by Thomas Dorr, had to be put down by state troops. Dorr himself was put in jail, but the state constitution was changed to reflect the demands of Dorr and his followers.

At first the Southern states refused to follow the North's lead in its advance toward universal suffrage. In fact many Southerners referred to universal male suffrage as, "the Northern plague." However, by the middle of the century, with the exception of blacks, the South too had generally adopted universal male suffrage.

On the eve of the Civil War almost all white men, both Northerners and Southerners, had the right to vote.

However, it took the Civil War to extend voting rights to blacks as well. President Lincoln had said: "In America up to now all men are created equal, except for Negroes." The Civil War, at least, began to change this situation.

Black Suffrage and Postwar Reconstruction

During and shortly after the end of the Civil War three important amendments to the U.S. Constitution were ratified. In 1865, the Thirteenth Amendment officially abolished slavery. The Fourteenth Amendment, adopted in 1868, guaranteed all citizens equality and civil rights. The Fifteenth Amendment, which became a part of the Constitution in 1870, gave blacks the right to vote.

The passage of these laws was one thing. Just as was later the case with the Prohibition Amendment, making it work was something else again.

Immediately after the war it became obvious that even though the South had lost the fight to maintain slavery it had no intention of doing away with white supremacy. Blacks were to continue in their roles as servants and poorly-paid field hands and laborers under their white masters. Certainly giving blacks the opportunity to vote was the farthest thought from most Southerners' minds.

The Black Codes

Some 4 million Southern slaves were freed as a result of the Civil War. With the rapid withdrawal of Union troops from the South when the war ended, many Southerners feared that these freedmen would rise up in bloody revolt. This never came close to happening, of course. One reason is that most of the freedmen were too busy trying to keep from starving to death. Also, many were searching throughout the South for their war-scattered families. Nevertheless, the South adopted "protective measures" called Black Codes that were all too similar to the earlier Slave Codes.

Under the Black Codes the freed slaves could not vote or serve on juries. They were also compelled to work no matter what wages or working conditions were provided. A refusal to do so could mean being put in jail on vagrancy charges. All blacks had to live in certain specified areas. They could not own firearms, and it was also illegal to "insult" white people. An insult could mean anything a white man said it meant.

The Freedmen's Bureau

In an attempt to help Southern blacks, Congress created the Freedmen's Bureau in 1865. This bureau helped the recently-freed blacks find homes, reunite with their families, and get jobs. It also attempted to protect them from abuse and exploitation. In 1866 Congress gave the bureau authority to protect blacks' voting rights and to set up schools for the freedmen.

In the North, President Andrew Johnson, who took office after President Lincoln was assassinated, opposed the Freedmen's Bureau. In the South, its activities were severely criticized. Southerners claimed the bureau turned blacks against their former masters. Freedmen schools were burned and the lives of white teachers from the North were threatened, driving many of them out of the South. Nevertheless, the bureau continued its work. By 1871 there were two hundred fifty thousand blacks enrolled in eleven colleges and universities and hundreds of other schools.

Had Lincoln lived to guide postwar Reconstruction, the lot of the Southern freedmen might have been better. But this is not necessarily so. Lincoln's postwar plans included being extremely generous about letting those states that had seceded back into the Union. All they had to do was declare their loyalty to the Union and the United States Constitution. Also, he did no more than suggest that perhaps "the very intelligent" blacks should be allowed to vote. Lincoln's greatest mistake may have been to make no plans for providing the freedmen with any property of their own or any opportunity to obtain it. Many blacks expected "forty acres and a mule" at the end of the war. When they did not get it, they had few choices other than to go to work for their former masters under what were often slavery-like conditions.

President Johnson was even more lenient than Lincoln toward the white South. To get back into the Union all a state had to do was establish a government and write a constitution. Needless to say, all of the new Southern state governments established under Johnson were white, and their constitutions said nothing about black civil rights or letting the freedmen vote. In fact, Johnson vetoed one civil rights bill and was opposed to the Fourteenth Amendment.

Congress Continues to Protect the Freedmen

Congress was not as lenient as either Lincoln or Johnson. In fact, it would not recognize the Southern state governments established while Lincoln and Johnson were in office. Congress also refused to seat the representatives and senators sent to Washington, D.C., by these new states. Instead it passed the First Reconstruction Act in 1867 which established Northern military rule in the South.

Johnson also vetoed this act. Congress made a futile attempt to remove Johnson from office by impeaching him. When this failed, Congress passed the Reconstruction Act over Johnson's veto. Out of it grew the Fourteenth and Fifteenth Amendments.

Under this act the right to vote was taken away from white Southerners who had fought against the North in the Civil War. Blacks, Southerners who had remained loyal to the Union, and Northerners living in the South were allowed to vote.

These provisions created one of the most controversial periods in American history. It was a time when many people said that not only blacks who could neither read nor write but also evil "carpetbaggers" and "scalawags" ruled the South. Basically, this was not true. However, this fiction has largely been carried over into modern times.

Carpetbaggers and Scalawags

To begin with, no Southern state legislatures were controlled by blacks at any time. Only in the lower house of the South Carolina legislature did blacks have a majority, and this was for only a brief period of time. There were indeed a few illiterate blacks elected to state legislatures, but these men were greatly outnumbered by those who were extremely capable and enacted much progressive legislation during the Reconstruction period. They included Jonathan J. Wright, who had been a prominent Pennsylvania lawyer before the war; Robert B. Elliott, who had been educated at England's Eton College; Hiram R. Revels, a top graduate of Knox College; John R. Lynch, a professional photographer and political leader, and numerous others.

As for the carpetbaggers and scalawags, not all of them were bad either. Carpetbaggers were supposedly unscrupulous Northerners who came into the South to take advantage of the chaotic postwar period. They carried all of their worldly goods in a suitcase or traveling bag made out of pieces of carpet. Thus, the name carpetbaggers was derived. Scalawags were Southern whites who worked for the Freedmen's Bureau or were otherwise pro-black.

Some carpetbaggers were indeed nothing more than adventurers out to make lots of quick money. But here again the bad apples were outnumbered by the good. A number of honest, well-meaning businessmen came down from the North to start new industries in

44

the South. Two such men were John T. Wilder and Willard Warner of Ohio. They started successful iron foundries in Birmingham, Alabama, and Chattanooga, Tennessee. Among the scalawags were three outstanding former Confederate Army officers, General James Longstreet and Colonels J. A. Alcorn and R. W. Flournoy.

Gains Under Congressional Reconstruction

Under Congressional Reconstruction the South was divided into five military districts. Each was headed by a military governor. These governors reported not to President Johnson but to Commander in Chief of the United States Army, Ulysses S. Grant. Their job was to maintain peace and order, enroll voters based on universal male suffrage—white and black—and to oversee the drafting of new state constitutions that included provisions for universal male suffrage.

By 1870 reconstructionist governments had been set up in all of the Southern states, and all had ratified the Fourteenth and Fifteenth Amendments to the U.S. Constitution. They were then formally readmitted to the Union and their representatives and senators were seated in the U.S. Congress. By 1872 an amnesty act was passed restoring the right to vote to all white men who had served in the Confederate Army during the Civil War.

Much other progress was also made in the South under Congressional Reconstruction before all federal troops were withdrawn. The infamous Black Codes were repealed, war-damaged roads and buildings were repaired, and countless new buildings, including schools, were built. In addition, free public education for all children was established throughout the South. Nevertheless, schools were racially segregated.

Southern Terrorist Organizations

None of this progress was made, however, without constant opposition. Much of it was violent too. Secret terrorist organizations were formed in the South in an effort to maintain white supremacy. Their main goal was to prevent blacks from voting.

The most notorious of these secret terrorist organizations was the Ku Klux Klan. Others included the Red Shirts, the Regulators, the White League, and the Knights of the White Camelia. All of these groups engaged in the worst kinds of terrorist tactics. Their activities can only be compared with those used later by Adolf Hitler's storm troopers in Nazi Germany before and during World War II. Blacks were injured, whipped, and lynched. Many of their white "nigger loving" sympathizers received the same treatment. Many whites who did not belong to these secret organizations, nevertheless, gave them quiet support by refusing to act

46

against them. They too did not want integrated state governments. They wanted governments run by white men.

The Ku Klux Klan (KKK) was formed as a social club in Pulaski, Tennessee, at the end of the Civil War by several former Confederate Army officers. General Nathan Bedford Forrest was its first leader or "Grand Wizard." Other KKK leaders included former Confederate General John B. Gordon and the former Governor of North Carolina, Zebulon B. Vance.

As soon as the North began Congressional Reconstruction in the South, the KKK changed from a social club into a terrorist organization bent on overthrowing Reconstruction state governments. KKK groups quickly sprang up throughout the South. Linking up with other similar groups, it formed "The Invisible Empire."

At first Klansmen contented themselves with intimidating blacks and their allies from voting by riding about the countryside at night wearing hooded white robes. These ghostly figures on horseback frequently frightened superstitious and poorly educated former slaves. They were further intimidated by the crosses the Klan would erect and set on fire in fields and on nearby hilltops. As the strength of the Reconstruction governments grew, however, the Klan resorted to more severe terrorist methods. Blacks' homes were burned and their occupants were murdered. In one year alone, 1871, almost two hundred blacks were lynched in just one Florida county, and more than three hundred were murdered near New Orleans.

In time, several state governments attempted to

47

act against the KKK and hundreds of suspects were arrested. However, few went to trial for violating the right of blacks to vote and even fewer were convicted. Almost none were prosecuted for murder. The North made some military efforts to stop Klan terrorism, but the guerrilla methods of the masked nightriders were more than a match for traditional army tactics. The failure to suppress these and other activities by white supremacists eventually led to the downfall of the Reconstruction state governments.

Reconstruction Ends

Ulysses S. Grant was elected United States president in 1868. When he took office in 1869, he immediately began to urge Congress to take further action to protect Southern blacks' voting and civil rights. The results were the passage in 1870 and 1871 of two pieces of legislation called, "Force Acts." These acts authorized the use of additional military power to enforce the Fourteenth and Fifteenth Amendments to the U.S. Constitution.

It soon became apparent, however, that the nation was no longer interested in Reconstruction. The public felt that the Civil War was over and maintaining an army of occupation in the South was pointless and expensive as far as taxes were concerned. Gradually, U.S. Army garrisons were eliminated in almost all of the

Southern states, and almost immediately white supremacists recaptured control of the state governments. By 1877, white rule was reestablished throughout the South.

Nevertheless, great gains—at an enormous cost in money and blood—had been made in obtaining black suffrage. Throughout the South, blacks continued to vote in great numbers, and some were elected to state legislatures. After U.S. Army troops were removed, the Ku Klux Klan and other terrorist organizations were no longer active. Relations between the white and black races improved. Whites and blacks freely intermingled in public gathering places, on public transportation, in restaurants, and in amusement centers such as theaters. This state of affairs continued for the next twenty years. Then, with a powerful rebirth of white supremacy, "Jim Crow" segregation laws were established throughout the South and equal rights for blacks were again ignored (see the section on civil rights later in this book).

Unfortunately, after the downfall of the state Reconstruction governments many of the more radical white supremacists had merely temporarily gone underground. This was indicated by the fact that there were still occasional lynchings of blacks in rural areas as well as other continuing attempts to intimidate blacks from voting. Gradually, these attempts at intimidation increased. As a result, for the next hundred years blacks and their white allies would have to continue their fight to prove that the Fifteenth Amendment, which gave blacks the right to vote, was worth more than the paper it was printed on.

49

Gradually, the barriers to blacks voting in both the North and South have been broken down. Attempts to prevent blacks from voting by the use of poll taxes, literacy tests, and other voter qualification tests have been set aside by amendments to the U.S. Constitution and history-making decisions by the Supreme Court.

Since the passage of the Twenty-fourth Amendment barring poll taxes in 1964, and the Voting Rights Act of 1965, blacks have been more successful at being able to vote and getting elected to office than they have been at any time since Reconstruction. In 1970 more than five hundred fifty blacks were elected to office in eleven Southern states. By 1976 this number had increased to almost two thousand. However, blacks still make up less than 3 percent of elected Southern officeholders, although they make up more than 20 percent of the South's population.

So the battle for black suffrage continues right up to the present day.

Women's Suffrage and Women's Rights

The women's suffrage movement also made its greatest gains after the Civil War. However, it would take until well into the next century before women actually got the vote.

There had been some effort on the part of women to obtain suffrage since colonial times, but it had met with only limited success. New Jersey's original state constitution did give women the right to vote, but this right was later withdrawn. It was not until about 1830 that women really began to agitate for suffrage.

In the 1830s many women went to work in factories and thus, as a group, became an important part of the work force. This made their demand for equal rights with men more powerful. Their leaders worked with men who were seeking changes not only in the voting laws but also in laws regarding education, religion, and the abolition of slavery. At many of the meetings held to discuss these public issues, and especially at antislavery meetings, women spoke out for both black suffrage and women's suffrage.

First Women's Suffrage Movement

A New England woman, Lucretia Coffin Mott, was one of the important leaders in the campaign against slavery and for equal rights for women. She was born of Quaker parents in Massachusetts in 1793. After graduating from a Quaker boarding school she became a teacher. Later she helped found the American Anti-Slavery Society.

In 1840, Lucretia Coffin Mott attended a world antislavery conference in London, but the conference refused to seat women delegates. While in London she met another American delegate, Elizabeth Cady Stan-

51

ton. The two women planned a women's rights convention to be held in the United States. The convention was held at Seneca Falls, New York, in 1848. At this meeting the first women's suffrage movement in the United States was launched with a declaration that was modeled after the Declaration of Independence. Written by Elizabeth Cady Stanton, the declaration said that "all men and women are created equal" but that "the history of mankind is a history of repeated injuries and usurpations on the part of man toward women." It ended with a demand that as a first step toward equal rights women should be given the right to vote.

Postwar Growth Toward Women's Suffrage

After the Civil War the "suffragettes" continued to gain ground in their fight for suffrage, although often it was in the face of male ridicule. Suffragette leaders strongly objected to both the Fourteenth and Fifteenth Amendments to the U.S. Constitution because they did not include giving suffrage to women. They disagreed, however, on what steps should be taken next. Some wanted a women's suffrage amendment added to the federal Constitution, and others wanted such an amendment added to all state constitutions.

In 1869 the disagreement led to the formation of the National Woman Suffrage Association (NWSA) by Elizabeth Cady Stanton and Susan B. Anthony, the temperance leader. A second organization, the American Woman Suffrage Association (AWSA), was headed by Lucy Stone, who was said to be the first woman lecturer on women's rights. She was also one of the first, if not the first, married women to keep her maiden name.

In 1890, NWSA and AWSA united as the National American Woman Suffrage Association with Elizabeth Cady Stanton as its first president. Lucy Stone served as head of the executive committee. Later, Susan B. Anthony, Carrie Chapman Catt, and Dr. Anna Howard Shaw also served as presidents of the organization. These women and numerous others vigorously pressed the fight for women's suffrage and women's rights.

Beginning in 1878 a women's suffrage amendment to the Constitution was regularly presented to every U.S. Congress, but it was always voted down. In the West several territories and states were the first to grant women the right to vote. The Wyoming Territory was the first to do so in 1869. The Utah Territory quickly followed suit in 1870, and then Colorado and Idaho also did so in 1893 and 1896, respectively. By the outbreak of World War I, however, only fifteen states offered full voting privileges to women. Twelve other states permitted women to vote in presidential elections, and two states permitted them to vote in primary elections. This left nineteen states in which women were still without any voting rights whatsoever.

World War I Brings Suffrage to Women

World War I caused a complete revolution in society's manners, morals, and lifestyles. It also caused something of a political revolution. During the war thousands of suffragettes rolled bandages and worked in hospitals, government offices, and factories. They felt they were taking part in the war effort on an equal basis with men. They demanded that they also share in the running of the country on an equal basis with men. Many other suffragettes were pacifists and blamed men for getting America into the war.

Of all of the nation's presidents up to this time only President Theodore Roosevelt in 1912 had advocated a constitutional amendment granting women the vote. However, during World War I it became apparent that politicians could no longer ignore the women's suffrage movement. Wartime President Woodrow Wilson was personally opposed to the suffrage crusade. Nevertheless, he decided—partly as a patriotic gesture to boost women's morale—to ask Congress for a new amendment to the Constitution giving women the vote.

President Wilson requested the amendment in September of 1918, just two months before World War I ended. The proposal was followed by long months of dramatic debate and action across the land. Suffragettes picketed the national capital, went on hunger strikes, and held parades and mass meetings to promote their cause. Many went to jail for disturbing the peace.

Finally, on June 4, 1919, Congress passed the

Nineteenth Amendment. It became the law of the land on August 26, 1920, when Tennessee became the thirty-sixth state to ratify the measure. More than 25 million American women had won the right to vote.

Soon after the Nineteenth Amendment was ratified, the National American Woman Suffrage Association joined the newly formed League of Women Voters to help educate women in political issues. They also worked with the National Woman's Party to add yet one more amendment to the U.S. Constitution. This amendment would provide complete equality of rights for women.

The Women's Liberation Movement

Following the suffrage victory of 1920, the women's equality movement was comparatively inactive for several decades. Then, just as had happened during the Civil War period, a renewed struggle for black civil rights and a new war caused the women's rights movement to again gain momentum.

In the 1960s many young women took part in protests against the continued white discrimination against blacks. They also protested America's involvement in Vietnam. Partly out of these protest activities and partly out of a renewed realization that society in general did not treat women on a fully equal basis with men, the Women's Liberation or "Women's Lib" movement was born. Its basic premise was that women should and must be dealt with as equal human beings. It also sought to show the absolute necessity for equal rights for *all* human beings.

In 1963 Betty Friedan wrote a book called *The Feminine Mystique*. In it Ms. Friedan noted that most Americans believed that a woman's place was in the home. Even college-educated women, she observed, often failed to use their training and resigned themselves to remaining at home as housewives and mothers. In 1966, Betty Friedan organized the National Organization for Women (NOW) to spearhead the activities of the Women's Liberation movement.

During the 1970s, interest in Women's Liberation became widespread. Child-care centers for professional working mothers were organized. Women's groups filed legal suits against sex discrimination. Others formed lobbies to petition Congress for new women's equality laws. The national media—radio, television, newspapers, magazines, and books—took up the Women's Liberation cause. Another book, this one by Kate Millett, became a best seller. In it Ms. Millett said that women should be treated as individuals, not as sex objects. Women, she added, did not want to be merely regarded as wives and mothers any more than men wanted to be merely regarded as husbands and fathers.

Finally, out of this continued agitation, a major victory was scored. This was the passage by Congress in 1972 of the Equal Rights Amendment (ERA), which, if ratified by the necessary thirty-eight states, would become the Twenty-seventh Amendment to the U.S. Constitution.

The Equal Rights Amendment

When the Equal Rights Amendment was submitted to the states for ratification in the spring of 1972, its quick approval seemed assured. But then it began to run into trouble with anti-ERA groups. Soon it was causing as much controversy as Prohibition's challenge to the U.S. Constitution had caused more than half a century earlier.

The amendment itself seemed innocent enough. But its fifty-two words created a furor. They were:

Section 1. Equality of rights under the law shall not be denied or abridged by the United States or by any State on account of sex.

Section 2. The Congress shall have the power to enforce, by appropriate legislation, the provisions of this article.

Section 3. This amendment shall take effect two years after the date of ratification.

Twenty-two state legislatures approved the amendment in 1972. Then, as opposition arose to the ERA, approval began to lag. Two states, Nebraska and Kentucky, later rescinded their ratification, although there was debate over whether a state could rescind ratification once it had granted it. By the late 1970s the ERA was still three states short of the necessary total of thirty-eight.

Unfortunately for the backers of the bill, there was a time limit within which ratification could occur. The deadline for adding the ERA to the U.S. Constitution was March 22, 1979. In October 1978, this original deadline was extended to June 30, 1982.

If the ERA Were Approved

Although the ERA sounded simple and innocent, there was little doubt that its passage would have a revolutionary impact on the whole of American society. Those who favored the measure said that these revolutionary changes would be for the good; those who opposed it said they would be bad.

Constitutional lawyers agreed that the ERA would directly affect family relations, military service, employment, property rights, education, and other areas as well.

In the area of family relations, most states have dual standards for the minimum marriage age for men and women. These would have to be changed. Wives

58

might not feel it necessary to adopt their husbands' surnames any longer. A woman's legal home would no longer necessarily be that of her husband's. In the case of divorce, men would no longer necessarily have to pay alimony, nor would they be mainly responsible for the support of their wives and children.

Military laws would have to be changed. Perhaps women in the military would be subject to combat duty on an equal basis with men.

Today, women comprise about 38 percent of the nation's labor force. They hold 33 percent of all professional, technical, and managerial positions. Under the ERA, these and future women workers would undoubtedly have the path cleared for them toward equal pay with men and promotions on an equal basis. Jobs now closed to women such as driving heavy trucks and mining would be opened. Under Social Security some changes would result that would benefit men. For example, a widower would be able to draw benefits just as a widow does today.

Many unmarried and divorced women today find it difficult to obtain financial credit with business establishments or banks. Under the ERA this situation would necessarily change.

Young women have long been discouraged from entering trade schools or engaging in interscholastic athletics such as basketball, baseball, and football. Constitutional lawyers claim that the ERA would open sports competition to physically qualified females. The claim by ERA opponents that young men and women would have to share the same locker rooms or rest rooms (as well as barracks and dormitories) is false. The constitutional right to privacy bars any such action.

Obviously, not all of these and numerous other changes would occur immediately. Even if the ERA were to be ratified immediately, there would be a two-year grace period during which state laws could be repealed or amended so they would be in line with the new law of the land. In addition, there would be many situations in which the new amendment would be challenged in the courts. Then, once again, it would be up to the Supreme Court to resolve this most recent challenge to the U.S. Constitution.

Civil Rights

The time: A few weeks before Christmas in 1955. The place: Montgomery, Alabama. The key person involved: Mrs. Rosa Parks, a forty-two-year-old black woman who was just about to be involved in an incident that would make modern civil rights history.

Mrs. Parks was a rather ordinary citizen to play such an important role. Certainly she never would have regarded herself as a heroine in the black civil rights drama or any other drama. Nevertheless, she was about to become one.

Mrs. Parks worked as a seamstress in a downtown Montgomery department store. When she got off work on the evening of December 1, she was tired and eager to get home. She boarded a bus at Court Square, the same square where slave auctions had been held just a century before.

The bus that Mrs. Parks boarded, like all Southern buses, was segregated. This meant that blacks sat in the back and whites in the front. If more whites got on than there were seats available for in front, then already seated blacks were expected to relinquish their seats in the back section. That was exactly what happened on this particular evening.

However, Mrs. Parks refused to give up her seat. She was bone-tired physically, and emotionally she was bone-tired of being treated like a second-class citizen in a segregated society.

"No," Mrs. Parks said when bus driver J. F. Blake told her to move. "No, I won't do it."

Bus driver Blake called the police, and Mrs. Parks was arrested for violating the segregation law. Later she was fined fourteen dollars, and the incident was briefly reported on a back page in the Montgomery daily newspaper, the *Advertiser*. Reading the item, Montgomery's white citizens were inclined to shrug their shoulders and observe that another "uppity nigger" had been put in her place.

But the incident didn't end there. Far from it.

First of all, on the evening Mrs. Parks was arrested, her $100 bail bond was signed by E. D. Nixon, the long-time leader of Montgomery's black community and former Alabama president of the National Association for the Advancement of Colored People (NAACP). Nixon was quick to realize that the Parks incident was one that could fan into flame the smouldering resentment of all blacks against the South's "Jim Crow" segregation laws.

62

The term Jim Crow for all blacks had been popularized early in the nineteenth century by a white entertainer, Thomas D. "Daddy" Rice. Rice, who wore blackface makeup to perform his act, was always on the lookout for new and novel black songs and dance routines. In Louisville, Kentucky, Rice saw a black stablehand do an odd little hopping kind of dance while he sang:

Wheel about and turn about
And do just so;

Every time I wheel about
I jump Jim Crow.

Rice incorporated the song and dance into his act, and the routine immediately became a worldwide hit. To most white Americans and many foreigners as well, from Rice's time on, Jim Crow came to mean a black person.

Nixon's method of using Rosa Parks' arrest to combat Jim Crow segregation laws was to organize a boycott of all of Montgomery's buses by Montgomery blacks. He also urged Mrs. Parks to fight her case in court. She agreed. This legal step was an important one because just a year earlier, in 1954, the Supreme Court had ruled that the segregation of public schools was unconstitutional. Any further legal gain that could be made by blacks, no matter how small, was one more nail in the coffin of Jim Crow.

On the face of it, a refusal by blacks to ride Mont-

gomery's buses did not seem to be a particularly powerful gesture. But blacks paid 75 percent of the city's bus
fares. A boycott that was 100 percent effective could
bankrupt the company.

Nixon knew that he alone could not organize the
city's blacks into a single unified force of resistance. For
this he needed a powerful leader. He asked the pastor of
a local Baptist church, Dr. Martin Luther King, Jr., if
he would aid the Montgomery bus boycott cause. When
King agreed, Nixon knew the cause was on the road to
victory.

Martin Luther King, Jr., was a champion of black
rights for the whole of his short life. Dr. King was born
in Atlanta, Georgia, in 1929, and died from an assassin's
bullet in Memphis, Tennessee, early in 1968. In his
short span of years, however, Dr. King was to become
a towering figure in the fight against not only racial
discrimination but also poverty and war. In 1964, he
would become the youngest man to be awarded the
Nobel peace prize.

The Montgomery bus boycott was King's first
major civil rights effort. While in school—he received
his Ph.D. degree in theology from Boston University—
King became interested in the teachings of Henry David
Thoreau and Mohandas K. Gandhi. Both these men
advocated the use of nonviolent resistance to obtain
political and social reform. King later wrote: "I came
to feel that nonviolent resistance was the only morally
and practically sound method open to oppressed people
in their struggle for freedom." In Montgomery, King's
beliefs were put to the test.

The organization that was formed to lead the bus boycott was called the Montgomery Improvement Association. King headed this organization. He spoke at black rallies and he and Nixon saw to it that the Montgomery *Advertiser* also heard about the boycott. Handbills were printed and distributed to the city's some forty thousand blacks.

The boycott began on December 5, 1955. On that morning Dr. Martin Luther King, Jr., stood on the steps of his Dexter Avenue Baptist Church and watched the first commuter buses of the day roll by. Not a single black was aboard. Not a single black boarded a bus in Montgomery that day. The first battle in the nonviolent war had been won. However, it did not remain a nonviolent war long—at least not on the part of Montgomery's whites.

While driving his car Dr. King was arrested on numerous occasions on trumped-up speeding charges. His home was bombed. King's response was to tell his angry followers to heed the Biblical command to love one's enemies. The lives and property of many other blacks were threatened, but their nonviolent resistance continued. Blacks walked to work or formed car pools and ran jitney taxis for transportation. Mass meetings continued to be held at which King cautioned his followers against violent retaliation and urged them on in their course of nonviolent resistance.

White resistance to bus desegregation also continued. Some of it was bitterly ironic. At least 70 percent of the city's working black women were maids and cleaning women for white families. To get them to and from work white men acted as the black women's chauffeurs. Since it was against the law for them to sit alongside a white man, the black women sat in the back seat to be driven to their jobs as maids. King later observed: "The white women of Montgomery wanted their black help more than they wanted to defy the boycott by firing them."

King and his followers also continued to fight for their cause in the courts. Rosa Parks lost her case and had to pay the fourteen dollar fine, but it was an empty victory for the segregationists. When she walked out of the courthouse, more than a thousand people stood outside cheering.

The Montgomery bus boycott continued for more than a year—actually 382 days. Then, in late 1956, the U.S. Supreme Court ruled that bus segregation was unconstitutional.

Dr. King, Vice-President Nixon, and the Reverend Ralph Abernathy rode together on the first desegregated bus to move through Montgomery's streets on December 21, 1956. If not dead, Jim Crow laws and stereotypes were dying.

About the bus boycott and its success, Dr. King said: "It proved there is a new Negro in the South, with a new sense of dignity and destiny."

Beginnings of the Civil Rights Movement

Actually, the civil rights movement began in the United States during post-Civil War Reconstruction. The key civil rights amendment added to the U.S. Constitution during this period was the Fourteenth. It not only guaranteed the right of racial equality but it also said that the federal government was responsible for protecting civil rights. Before that the states had this responsibility, and many of them totally disregarded it, especially in regard to blacks.

Unfortunately, however, the Fourteenth Amendment proved to be of little continuing help to the freed slaves. When Reconstruction ended, white supremacy returned to the South. Soon the civil rights protection clause of the Fourteenth Amendment was being almost completely ignored. While blacks were now citizens, they were second-class citizens at best.

With the rebirth of white supremacy came enforced racial separation. All the Southern states passed laws prohibiting racial intermarriage. Jim Crow laws were also passed segregating blacks and whites in public places and on public transportation. Public schools were also segregated.

In an attempt to add more muscle to the enforcement arm of the Fourteenth Amendment, Congress passed a Civil Rights Act in 1875. It specifically prohibited racial discrimination in inns or hotels, public conveyances, theaters, and other public amusement

67

places. However, the 1883 the Supreme Court declared that this law was unconstitutional.

Then, in 1896, the Supreme Court rendered another milestone decision that was to strike a virtual death blow to the black civil rights cause. This decision was handed down in the celebrated case called *Plessy v. Ferguson,* one of the most important cases in the history of the Supreme Court.

Plessy v. Ferguson

On July 10, 1890, the Louisiana state legislature passed a Jim Crow law requiring railroads to carry blacks in "separate but equal" railroad cars. The law was titled, "An Act to Promote the Comfort of Passengers."

In the black community of New Orleans there was some talk of boycotting the railroads—as was later done so successfully in the Montgomery bus situation—but nothing came of it. Black community leaders then decided to gather funds to test the law in the courts. They soon had collected more than fifteen hundred dollars.

The man selected as the lawyer to head the blacks' cause was Albion W. Tourgée. Tourgée's grandparents had been French Huguenots. He had fought with the Union Army during the Civil War and later had become a highly successful carpetbagger. Tourgée had championed the cause of the freedmen since the end of the war and was strongly opposed to segregation.

The man selected to test Louisiana's Jim Crow railroad-car law was a young black man named Homer Adolph Plessy. On June 7, 1892, Plessy boarded a train on the East Louisiana Railroad and took a seat in a white coach. Plessy was such a light-colored black that he could easily have passed as a white man. However, railroad officials had been alerted to the situation and were also eager to test the new law. They too were opposed to the law, not for civil rights reasons but because of the extra expense involved in providing separate cars for blacks and whites.

When Plessy was asked by the conductor to move to a Jim Crow coach, he refused. He was then arrested by Detective Christopher C. Cain. Plessy was brought before New Orleans Judge John H. Ferguson and charged with violating the Jim Crow railroad-car law. Tourgée entered a plea of not guilty for Plessy on grounds that the law violated the U.S. Constitution. Judge Ferguson ruled against Plessy, following which Tourgée appealed the case to the Louisiana State Supreme Court.

In the case that was now known as *Plessy v. Ferguson*, the state supreme court upheld Judge Ferguson's ruling and said the Jim Crow car law was valid. Tourgée then appealed the case to the U.S. Supreme Court.

In his brief to the Supreme Court, Tourgée pleaded that the segregation law violated the Fourteenth Amendment. He pointed out that "segregation perpetuates the worst aspects of slavery. The object of such a law," he continued, "is simply to debase and distinguish against a so-called inferior race. Its purpose has been properly interpreted by the general designation of 'Jim Crow Car' law. Its object is to separate the Negroes from the whites in public conveyances for the gratification of white superiority and white supremacy of power."

The Supreme Court did not hand down its decision in the case of *Plessy v. Ferguson* until 1896. Meanwhile, white supremacy had gained new strength in the South. Many new segregation laws had been passed. The number of black lynchings had greatly increased. The trend of the times was against supporting the cause of black civil rights. And the Supreme Court went along with this trend.

The Supreme Court handed down its decision on May 18, 1896. It supported Judge Ferguson's original ruling and declared that the separate but equal doctrine was a valid one. In short, the Court put its stamp of approval on the basic principle of segregation. To support its decision, the Supreme Court pointed out that Congress had already established segregated schools in the District of Columbia and that similar laws had been adopted by many state legislatures. These segregated school laws had all been sustained by the courts, so segregation on public conveyances was equally valid.

"The Constitution Is Color Blind"

One Supreme Court justice, however, strongly disagreed with his fellow justices in the case of *Plessy v. Ferguson*. This was John Marshall Harlan, a Southerner and former slaveholder. Known as the "Great Dissenter," Harlan's dissent in this case was loud and clear.

The Louisiana segregation law, he said, was in direct conflict with both the Fourteenth and Fifteenth Amendments. He went on: "The arbitrary separation of citizens, on the basis of race, is a badge of servitude wholly inconsistent with the public freedom and the equality before the law established by the Constitution. It cannot be justified upon any legal grounds. In the eye of the law, there is in this country no superior, dominant, ruling class of citizens. There is no caste here. *Our Constitution is color blind,* and neither knows nor tolerates classes among citizens. In respect of civil rights, all citizens are equal before the law."

However, it was not Justice Harlan's dissenting opinion that prevailed. It was the majority opinion of the Supreme Court that segregation was constitutional and therefore legal. This opinion would stand for more than half a century. Meanwhile, Jim Crow segregation laws were upheld by the Supreme Court. They would remain so until May 17, 1954. Then, the second black civil rights revolution since the Reconstruction era would begin to occur. This would be partially brought about by the Supreme Court's reversal of the *Plessy v. Ferguson* decision in its unanimous ruling in an epic

71

school desegregation case known as *Brown v. Board of Education of the City of Topeka.*

Brown v. Board of Education and The Role of the NAACP

During both World War I and World War II hundreds of thousands of blacks moved out of the South and into the North to work in the booming war factories. This mass migration proved to be both good and bad for the blacks. First of all, it gave many of them their first real independence that came from earning a substantial amount of money that they could call their own. Secondly, they found that their votes were important to Northern political leaders and that these votes could be traded for city jobs and other practical political favors.

Nevertheless, these migrant blacks soon learned that segregated conditions were virtually as bad in the North as they had been in the South. They were forced to live in ghettos, and whites in general regarded them with open hostility if they tried to take part in the "white" way of life. Jim Crow in the form of unwritten yet real discrimination against the blacks was still alive and well and living in the North.

The organization that did the most toward fighting discrimination and outright segregation was the National Association for the Advancement of Colored People (NAACP). Founded in 1909 after several race riots in Illinois, the NAACP soon became the "cutting edge" for the modern black civil rights movement. Its first chairman was Arthur B. Spingarn. Under Spingarn, the NAACP soon had more than one hundred thousand members who belonged to some four hundred chapters throughout the United States.

Originally, however, the NAACP did not concentrate on the fight against segregation. It centered its activities on eliminating lynchings and obtaining fair trials for blacks. It was during the great economic depression of the 1930s that the NAACP began to concentrate on the complete integration of American society.

Under President Franklin D. Roosevelt's New Deal program for improving economic conditions, blacks were given increasingly important consideration. Of the more than 12 million persons who were unemployed during the Great Depression it was the blacks who suffered most severely. Several of Roosevelt's New Deal relief measures were aimed directly at aiding these impoverished black members of the labor force.

Roosevelt's efforts were based partly on humanitarian and partly on political motives. He knew that he needed the big city vote to remain in office, and in many of the big cities in the North the blacks controlled the vote. Nevertheless, it was under the New Deal that blacks first obtained national political power. The NAACP was in the forefront of using this power to realize the blacks' history-long dream: full racial equality. The NAACP's method was to attack segregation in the courts.

73

"Mr. Civil Rights"

Probably the most important person to join the NAACP in the 1930s was Thurgood Marshall, a lawyer who has often been called, "Mr. Civil Rights." Marshall was born in Baltimore, Maryland, in 1908. He was destined to become the first black associate justice of the U.S. Supreme Court, in 1967. A graduate of Lincoln University in Pennsylvania and the Howard University Law School in Washington, D.C., Marshall became the general counsel of the NAACP Legal Defense and Education Fund in 1938. He was soon directing the use of $150,000 a year to fight desegregation cases throughout the country.

Marshall's strategy for attacking school segregation, especially in the South, was to attempt to force the admission of blacks into universities at the graduate school level. This strategy was based on the fact that it would be too expensive and too difficult for universities to provide "separate but equal" schools at the top level of education. As Oklahoma University President George L. Cross later admitted: "You can't build a cyclotron for one student." In addition, Southerners did not seem to object to school integration at the university level as much as they did at the primary and secondary levels.

Marshall and his colleagues won a single quick success. In 1938 the U.S. Supreme Court ruled that it violated the equal protection clause of the Fourteenth Amendment for the University of Missouri to refuse to allow a black student to enter its law school when there

74

were no separate but equal state law schools for him to attend.

World War II then put a temporary halt to all such litigation. However, after the war, lawsuits to force school integration began again. Cases similar to the one at the University of Missouri were brought to court in Oklahoma and Texas. The Oklahoma case differed somewhat in that the university officials there allowed a black student to enroll in its School of Education but then provided a "Reserved for Colored" section for him in classrooms, the library, and the dining hall. The U.S. Supreme Court struck down all such attempts at continued segregation.

Despite these and other victories, Marshall realized that nothing had really been accomplished by way of striking down the basic *Plessy v. Ferguson* decision that favored separate but equal public facilities of all kinds.

For a time the NAACP tried to get some of the Southern public school boards to adopt a process of "gradualism," that is, gradually allowing a few black children to enroll in white public schools. However, the South would have nothing to do with gradualism. Marshall and the NAACP then decided to "wage an all-out war in the courts against segregated schools."

75

Linda Brown's Case Goes to Court

In 1950 Marshall and his staff of NAACP lawyers filed five separate school segregation suits in various locations throughout the country: Topeka, Kansas; Clarendon County, South Carolina; Prince Edward County, Virginia; the state of Delaware; and the District of Columbia. All of these suits charged that not only were the black schools inferior to the white schools in the same area but that the separate but equal rule violated the protection clause of the Fourteenth Amendment. All of the suits were filed on behalf of elementary school children in each of the named areas. The suit in Topeka, Kansas, was filed on behalf of a black grade school student named Linda Brown.

Local courts all ruled that the *Plessy v. Ferguson* Supreme Court ruling was still valid and that separate but equal public school facilities were still legal. In several of the areas black school facilities were improved, but these were the only positive results that initially came from the suits. Then, in 1952, the Supreme Court agreed to hear and review all of the five cases. Linda Brown's case and all of the other similar cases, past and future, were finally going to have their day in court.

Marshall filed a brief for the NAACP. In addition, some thirty social scientists testified against school segregation, claiming that segregation did harm to *both* black and white children. John W. Davis, a constitutional lawyer who had run for president in 1924, presented a brief for the school boards in favor of continued segregation. His arguments were mainly based on precedent—the past law of the land—and its continued validity.

Six months passed before any word was heard from the Supreme Court. Then word came down that the Supreme Court wanted to have the cases retried before it on the basis of what the United States Congress had had in mind regarding school segregation when it passed the Fourteenth Amendment.

Marshall then called on a number of social scientists—mainly historians—to help him prepare this second brief. These historians spent several months in painstaking historical research, and turned all of it over to Marshall. Finally, on November 15, 1953, Marshall filed his second brief, which was accompanied by an enormous amount of historical documentation. The brief itself, however, was short and clear. It simply said:

The evidence makes clear that it was the intent of the proponents of the Fourteenth Amendment that it could, of its own force, prohibit all state action based upon race or color and all segregation in public education. The "separate but equal" rule of *Plessy v. Ferguson* was conceived in error and should be reversed forthwith. Moreover, any delay in executing the judgment of the Court would involve insurmountable difficulties so that the plaintiff children in question should be admitted at once without distinctions of race or color to the schools of their choice.

Attorney General Herbert Brownell filed a brief for the U.S. Department of Justice. Somewhat surprisingly, Brownell's brief said that the U.S. government favored desegregation but requested a transition period before it went into effect. The various school boards involved, with the exception of that in Topeka, once again resorted to the historical precedent of segregated schools being the accepted law of the land. The Topeka School Board came forth with a second surprise when it announced that it was voluntarily desegregating its schools.

Finally, on May 17, 1954, the Supreme Court handed down its unanimous decision. It was read by Chief Justice Earl Warren. In it Warren said, in part, that the historical question could not now be decided, but that today, in the twentieth century, "school segregation by state law causes a feeling of inferiority in black children that inflicts damage to their hearts and minds that may never be undone. Public school segregation by state law, therefore, violates the equal protection clause of the Fourteenth Amendment." He added finally: "The old *Plessy* separate but equal rule is herewith formally overruled."

Marshall and the NAACP had undoubtedly scored their greatest victory, but it was not a total victory. In its 1954 decision the Supreme Court did not order the immediate desegregation of schools. Instead, a year later, it added a follow-up ruling that ordered desegregation to be carried out by local federal courts "with all deliberate speed." Nevertheless, among all of the great challenges to the U.S. Constitution, *Brown v. Board of*

Education had proved to be one of the landmark Supreme Court decisions.

Controversy and the Court

Following its desegregation decisions of 1954 and 1955, a storm of national protest, especially in the South, arose against the Supreme Court. Controversy and the Court were not strangers. From the days of John Marshall until the present there have been occasions when the public has violently protested some action involving the Court. This is not surprising, of course, since the Supreme Court is the national umpire for interpreting the law of the land. Each of its major decisions is something like an umpire's decision in a hard-fought baseball world series. Such a decision is bound to make somebody angry.

Before the civil rights decisions of 1954 and 1955, another decision involving a black person's rights had angered Northerners in 1857. This was rendered in the *Dred Scott* case. Scott was a slave whose master had taken him out of the South into territory that had been declared free by the Missouri Compromise of 1820. Later Scott returned to the South where he claimed he was no longer a slave because he had lived in free territory. When his case reached the Supreme Court the Court declared Scott was still a slave and not a citizen and therefore had no rights at all. The decision also said that Congress had no power to prohibit slavery in the nation's territories and thus the Missouri Compromise was unconstitutional.

There were many Northerners who claimed that the Supreme Court's ruling in the *Dred Scott* case was largely responsible for starting the Civil War. Also, there were many Southerners who claimed that the Court's school desegregation decision of 1954 and its follow-up ruling in 1955 might start a new Civil War.

"Impeach Earl Warren" signs began to appear on bumper stickers and on signs across the country. These signs were accompanied by massive resistance to school desegregation. In many areas white students simply dropped out of public schools and reenrolled in white private schools. White citizens councils were formed in the South. These councils used not only legal maneuvers to prevent school desegregation but also resorted to violence. White mobs rioted in Little Rock, Arkansas, and its Central High School was temporarily closed when black students were admitted in 1957. James Meredith's attempt to enroll in the University of Mississippi in 1962 also caused violence and bloodshed.

Nevertheless, the Supreme Court did not back away from its desegregation stand. In fact, it went a step further. It declared that segregation on all public beaches and public golf courses, when such public facilities were maintained by a state or city, was illegal. It was at this time also that the Court declared illegal the segregation of city buses in Montgomery, Alabama.

"*Freedom Now*"

Having attained national stature as a civil rights leader in the Montgomery bus boycott, Dr. Martin Luther King, Jr., was at the forefront of the demonstrations marking the centennial anniversary of the Emancipation Proclamation in 1963. Although Lincoln's Proclamation in 1863 had in theory freed the blacks from slavery, few blacks thought they had truly experienced freedom in the hundred years since then. Blacks had adopted the slogan "Freedom Now" for the centennial year and were holding civil rights demonstrations throughout the South. They held lunch counter "sit-ins" to force the desegregation of public eating places. They had gone on "freedom rides" to defy segregation on interstate buses. They had gone on "freedom marches" to demonstrate for equal rights of all kinds. (On one such march between Memphis, Tennessee, and Jackson, Mississippi, James Meredith would be shot but would still manage to complete the march.) They had defied "white only" elections and forced their way onto the ballot and into polling places. In the spring of 1963 they planned a major nonviolent centennial rally and march through the streets of Birmingham, Alabama, a notorious stronghold of white supremacy.

Television cameras from all the major networks were focused on this Birmingham march which was led by Dr. King. Television viewers throughout the nation and the world were shocked when Birmingham police, led by their Chief Eugene "Bull" Connor, used police

81

dogs, firehoses, and billy clubs to break up the march. There were mass arrests of blacks as a result of this demonstration. One of those arrested was Dr. King. His arrest resulted in a moving letter he wrote to several local white clergymen who had protested his actions. In his "Letter From a Birmingham Jail" King pointed out that many African and Asian nations were gaining their political independence while "we still creep at a horse and buggy pace toward gaining a cup of coffee at a lunch counter."

On June 11, President John F. Kennedy addressed the nation on television regarding the events in Birmingham and elsewhere in the South. He said: "One hundred years of delay have passed since President Lincoln freed the slaves, yet their heirs, their grandsons are not fully free. They are not yet freed from the bonds of injustice; they are not yet freed from social and economic oppression.

"Now the time has come for this nation to fulfill its promise. The events in Birmingham and elsewhere have so increased the cries for equality that no city or state or legislative body can prudently choose to ignore them."

Later, in the fall of 1963, four black girls were killed when a bomb was thrown into a Birmingham church. Nobody was convicted of this crime until fourteen years later. In November 1977 Robert Chambliss, a former Ku Klux Klan member, was sentenced to life imprisonment for the murders.

Also in 1963 there was a march on Washington, D.C. At the foot of the Lincoln memorial, King addressed some two hundred fifty thousand civil rights marchers in his now-famous "I Have a Dream" speech. The final words, taken from an old slave song, were inscribed on his Atlanta gravesite monument following his assassination on April 4, 1968. They were:

Free at Last,
Free at Last,

Thank God Almighty,
I'm Free at Last!

As a direct result of King's efforts and those of his co-leaders in the civil rights movement, several civil rights laws were passed by Congress. These laws were a sign that the national conscience had been partially aroused by such events as nonviolent marchers having dogs and firehoses turned loose against them. The national conscience had been fully aroused by the assassination of President Kennedy in November of 1963 at Dallas, Texas. Kennedy had proposed a broad civil rights program but little of it had been passed. Following Kennedy's death, President Lyndon B. Johnson urged its passage by Congress and Congress did so—at least partially out of regard for the martyred young Kennedy.

These new laws were as important to the civil rights movement as any passed since the Reconstruction era. They included the Civil Rights Acts of 1964 and 1968 and the Voting Rights Act of 1965.

The Civil Rights Act of 1964 was aimed at protecting the right to equality in public accommodations, the right to have federal funds spent without racial discrimination, and the right to racial and sexual equality in employment. In order to make sure that this act would be upheld by the Supreme Court (it was similar to the act that had been declared unconstitutional in 1875), it was not based on the Fourteenth Amendment but on the clause in the U.S. Constitution giving Congress the power to regulate commerce. Regarding this aspect of the new law, Chief Justice Warren said: "It is rather a sad commentary on the development of the Fourteenth Amendment doctrine that Congress felt compelled to equate Negro rights with the movement of goods to enact civil rights legislation." Nevertheless, this device has enabled the law to remain on the statute books since it was passed. The following two acts have also been unanimously upheld by the Supreme Court: the Civil Rights Act of 1968, which prohibited racial discrimination in housing, and the Voting Rights Act of 1965 (extended in 1970), which eliminated *all* discriminatory qualifying tests for people who want to register to vote. This act also provided for the appointment of federal officials, where necessary, to register voters. This has prevented any possible local discrimination, and has made the Fifteenth Amendment worth considerably more than the paper it was written on.

Civil Rights Today

Although "black evangelism" and the second civil rights revolution of the 1950s and 1960s scored great gains for blacks throughout the nation, these gains have yet to be fully consolidated. In the late 1960s and early 1970s the "Black Power" movement—a phrase first used by Stokely Carmichael of the Student Nonviolent Coordination Committee (SNCC) in 1966 during a civil rights march in Mississippi—was a step in the direction of consolidating black gains. Black Power symbolizes the efforts by American black people to gain their maximum political and economic power. It also expresses the pride of American blacks in their African heritage.

It is in the economic area that American blacks are probably still suffering most from discrimination today. Before his assassination Martin Luther King, Jr., organized the Poor People's Campaign to dramatize the poverty that still afflicted America's blacks in the late 1960s. King's death and the national preoccupation with the Vietnam War until its end in 1975 kept the national conscience from being aroused about black economic discrimination as it had earlier been aroused over black civil rights discrimination. That situation still exists today, more than a decade after Dr. King's death.

As one black civil rights worker has commented: "It's not a question of a black being able to check into a first-class motel today. It's a question of being able to

85

afford to check out." Others have said: "What good is a seat in the front of the bus if you don't have the money for bus fare?"

Throughout the land, but perhaps especially in the South, an enormous difference in white and black employment rates and salary scales exists. Census figures compiled by the Southern Regional Council show that in the South, white median income (half of the employed earned more, and half less) in 1968 was $9,240, while the black median income was $5,226. By the late 1970s Southern whites were earning an annual median salary of $12,150 and blacks $6,240.

Unemployment figures for blacks in the South during the late 1970s were double those for whites. For blacks under twenty in Southern cities, unemployment ran as high as 35 percent.

National census figures show that for the U.S. as a *whole* in the late 1970s, the median income for black families was $8,779 as opposed to $14,268 for white families. Department of Labor officials said that the difference in earnings between the two groups was steadily growing. As a rude measure of the difference between the standards of living of whites and blacks, the American Friends Service Committee reported that according to one of their surveys seven out of ten blacks in rural Alabama were living in homes that had no indoor flush toilets.

Much indeed has been accomplished by the modern civil rights movement. However, in all too many instances, to be black in America today still means to be poor, under-educated, and socially excluded from the white community. It also often means living in a second-rate, segregated neighborhood and being excluded from employment on a completely equal basis with whites. Dr. King's "dream" has yet to be fully realized.

Criminal Justice and the Warren Court

The decision against school segregation was not the only decision to cause controversy to rage about the heads of Chief Justice Earl Warren and the other members of the Supreme Court. Their generally liberal rulings on civil rights violence and other types of "freedom of expression" were widely criticized. Obscenity laws were relaxed under the Warren Court, while it also ruled against religion in the public schools. The general public was not at all sure it liked this. However, the decisions that perhaps caused the most controversy were those that resulted in drastic changes in the criminal justice system.

For the first time, decisions by the Warren Court gave protection, under the Bill of Rights, to people accused of crimes not only in federal but also in state prosecution cases.

In 1961, in a case called *Mapp v. Ohio*, the Supreme Court ordered the release of an Ohio woman named Dollree Mapp because she had been convicted on the basis of obscene books, pictures, and drugs found in her home when the police searched it without a warrant. This, the Court said, was "illegal search and sei-zure" and unconstitutional under the Fourth Amendment of the Bill of Rights.

However, the case that really caught the public's attention was that of *Gideon v. Wainwright,* which reached the Supreme Court in 1963.

Gideon Blows His Trumpet

Clarence Gideon was a poor, middle-aged man who had been in and out of jail for a good part of his life. He had been convicted four times for felonies and the last time for a burglary in Florida. While in his Florida jail cell, Gideon wrote a letter to the U.S. Supreme Court. That letter proved to be a trumpet call to justice.

As U.S. Attorney General Robert F. Kennedy later said: "If an obscure Florida convict named Clarence Earl Gideon had not sat down in his prison cell with a pencil and paper to write a letter to the Supreme Court, and if the Court had not taken the trouble to look for merit in that one crude petition among all the bundles of mail it must receive every day, the vast machinery of American law would have gone undisturbed. But Gideon *did* write that letter, the Court *did* look into the case, and the whole course of American legal history has been changed."

Gideon's letter was a simple one. In it he referred to his "limited education and also the utter folly and hopelessness" of parts of his life. He further wrote: "My question is very simple. I requested the Florida court to appoint me an attorney and the court refused."

Since Gideon was too poor to hire his own lawyer and the court had not appointed one for him, Gideon was put on trial without anyone to defend him. He was found guilty and sent to jail. Under the law at this time the state of Florida had done nothing to violate the U.S. Constitution according to previous Supreme Court decisions.

However, the Supreme Court decided that Gideon's civil rights and civil liberties, regardless of the fact that he was a previously convicted felon, had been violated. In its decision in favor of Gideon's pencil-written petition the Court said: "Reason and reflection require us to recognize that in our adversary system of criminal justice, any person haled into court, who is too poor to hire a lawyer, cannot be assured a fair trial unless counsel is provided for him. This seems to be an obvious truth."

Gideon's conviction was reversed and he was acquitted at a second trial at which he *was* represented by counsel. More importantly, however, Gideon's letter had resulted in a Supreme Court decision that would affect thousands of future defendants and alter the course of the American criminal justice system.

Miranda v. Arizona

A second landmark decision in the criminal justice area was handed down by the Supreme Court in 1966 in the case of *Miranda v. Arizona*.

Ernesto Miranda had been arrested in Phoenix, Arizona, and charged with both rape and robbery. While he was in police custody, Miranda was subjected to severe and prolonged questioning. Finally, he signed a confession. This confession was used as evidence at Miranda's trial, and largely on the basis of it he was convicted.

In this instance there was no question of the defendant having a lawyer. Miranda had one all right, and it was he who protested that the use of Miranda's confession to convict him violated the Fifth Amendment of the Bill of Rights. This amendment says that a person cannot be compelled to incriminate himself. Miranda's confession, his lawyer claimed, had been forced out of him and thus he had been forced to incriminate himself.

On June 13, 1966, the Supreme Court handed down its ruling reversing Miranda's conviction based on the grounds that it was indeed obtained in violation of the Bill of Rights. But in presenting the majority opinion of the Court, Chief Justice Warren went a step further in protecting the rights of criminal suspects. Justice Warren said: "Unless other fully effective means are devised to inform accused persons of their right of silence and to assure a continuous opportunity to exercise it, the following measures are required: Prior to any questioning, the person must be warned that he has a right to remain silent, that any statement he does make may be used as evidence against him, and that he has a right to the presence of an attorney, either retained or appointed. The defendant may waive effectuation of these rights, provided the waiver is made voluntarily, knowingly, and intelligently. If, however, he indicates in any manner and at any stage of the process that he wishes to consult with an attorney before speaking, there can be no questioning. Likewise, if the individual is alone and indicates in any manner that he does not wish to be interrogated, the police may not question him. The mere fact that he may have answered some questions or volunteered some statements on his own does not deprive him of the right to refrain from answering any further inquiries until he has consulted with an attorney and thereafter consents to be questioned."

Objections to the Warren Court's Criminal Justice Decisions

There has been widespread criticism, especially by the police and other law-enforcement agencies, of these and numerous other similar rulings by the Warren Court in the criminal justice area. They have claimed that these decisions, and especially the one in the *Miranda* case, give undue protection to suspects and make investigation and conviction much more difficult than in the past. Police officials point out that the severe rise in crime can only be brought to a halt if enforcement measures are helped, not hindered. They add that they have been given little additional help from the Supreme Court by way of protecting society, although the Supreme Court has bent over backwards to assure criminals and suspected criminals of their rights. Some critics have even said that criminals are being pampered while their innocent victims are being ignored.

Recently, there has been some indication that public opinion may cause the Supreme Court to modify its earlier criminal justice decisions. In the past, time has seemed to temper the Court's opinions and caused the pendulum of justice to swing back when it has swung either too far to the left or right. This no doubt will again happen in the future.

Religious Freedom

One of the ironic things about a number of the early American colonists was the fact that they fled Europe to seek religious freedom, but in the New World they proceeded to make those who disagreed with their worship of God outcasts. Certain civil liberties and civil rights—suffrage, for example—were denied to those who belonged to different religious denominations or to none at all. In some instances this religious intolerance and fanaticism became outright persecution. Such was the case of the witchcraft trials at Salem, Massachusetts.

Ignorant and superstitious people have often believed in witches. This belief has usually taken the place of the more formal and humanitarian religious beliefs of better-educated and more cosmopolitan people. As late as the seventeenth century in Europe, however, people were still persecuting "witches." These "witches"

93

were usually women who, it was said, had sold their souls to the devil. In Germany and France several thousand suspected witches were put to death. Several hundred were also killed in England.

This witch-hunting hysteria spread from England to America in 1692. Witches were persecuted in several of the colonies, but the trials reached their peak in Salem and Salem Village (today's Danvers), Massachusetts. There, half a dozen little girls began barking like dogs and otherwise behaving strangely. They told their parents that Tituba, a slave from the West Indies who was owned by the Reverend Samuel Parris, had bewitched them. Actually, Tituba had been telling the little girls harmless voodoo tales of Tituba's native country in the Caribbean.

Nevertheless, the witchcraft hysteria spread swiftly. It was encouraged by another colonial preacher, Cotton Mather, who told the colonists that their children had been bewitched because of the sinful way of life that too many of them were leading. The wave of hysteria lasted for eight months, during which time 150 colonists were jailed and 19 were put to death. The trials, which were held before Judge Samuel Sewall, were the last held for witchcraft in the colonies.

Unfortunately, however, an atmosphere similar to that surrounding the Salem witchcraft trials has often continued to accompany the search for religious tolerance and understanding in America right up to the present day.

94

The First Amendment

The Founding Fathers knew that religious freedom could be one of the first and most important challenges to the U.S. Constitution. That was why they included reference to it in the very first of the ten amendments to the Constitution which make up the Bill of Rights.

The Founding Fathers did not, of course, make up the Bill of Rights out of the whole cloth. Before the U.S. Constitution was written, the original thirteen colonies, having learned by early and bitter experience, had gotten around to creating their own charters of liberty. They then demanded that a similar charter be added to the Constitution. This became our Bill of Rights, which is the cornerstone of American democracy. It begins:

Congress shall make no law respecting an establishment of religion, or prohibiting the free exercise thereof; or abridging the freedom of speech, or of the press. . . .

Mainly because of the foresight of the Founding Fathers in writing the First Amendment to the U.S. Constitution, the Supreme Court, until recently, has had to respond to few challenges regarding religious freedom. The First Amendment, for example, made it illegal to establish any government-supported or official state religion. In Europe, religious wars had gone on for hundreds of years with various kings trying to establish and maintain the churches of their choice. In America, the Constitution was "king" and it said that the people could establish and support the churches of their choice. Or, they did not have to support any church at all, if that was their choice. This came to be known as the separation of church and state.

The Scopes "Monkey Trial"

In modern times, when conflicts between church and state have occurred, they have usually occurred in the public schools. Such was the case that led to the Scopes "Monkey Trial" in Tennessee in 1925. Although this trial took place in the twentieth century, the hysterical atmosphere that surrounded it was similar to that of the Salem witchcraft trials.

Twenty-four-year-old John T. Scopes was the defendant in this trial. He was a teacher in Dayton, Tennessee. In his classroom, young Scopes taught Darwin's theory of the evolution of plants, animals, and man. This theory is based on the concept of natural selection. This was against Tennessee state law which "prohibited the teaching in any public school any theory that denies the story of the divine creation of man as taught in the Bible, and to teach instead that man has descended from a lower order of animals." What this law and Scopes' arrest on the basis of it implied was that Scopes was teaching that man had descended from the monkey. Scopes strongly denied this, and it was not what Darwin had meant either.

However, the trial did not really center on whether or not Scopes was teaching atheism disguised as science. What it centered on was an attempt to force Scopes and all other Tennessee teachers to deny modern knowledge to their students in favor of Fundamental religious dogma or unsubstantiated opinion.

The attorney for the prosecution was the Cotton Mather of his day, William Jennings Bryan. Also the greatest orator of his day, Bryan had unsuccessfully run for the presidency three times and had served as secretary of state under Woodrow Wilson. A religious Fundamentalist himself, Bryan claimed to know the Bible by heart.

Clarence Darrow was the attorney for the defense. Darrow was an avowed agnostic and the most famous criminal lawyer in the United States. Author and news-paperman Lincoln Steffens called Darrow "the attorney for the damned," because he had defended so many poor and unfortunate clients. Certainly Darrow was the legal champion of the common people and as such did not like self-righteous, pompous people—and he regarded Bryan as just that.

The trial was held all during the searing hot month of July. Air conditioning had not been invented yet, and the extreme conditions turned the trial into more of a circus than a formal proceeding in a court of law. One newspaper reporter wrote that it was "hard to know whether Dayton was holding a carnival or a belated Fourth of July celebration. Literally, it was drunk on religious excitement."

Scopes' opponents strung a banner across the courtroom that read: "Read Your Bible Daily." Darrow demanded equal space for a sign. His read: "Read Your Evolution Daily."

When the trial began the judge called for a local preacher to give the Divine blessing. Darrow objected that this was unconstitutional. His objection was overruled. Thereafter, prayers were read at the start of each day's session.

What soon became apparent was that not Scopes but Bryan's Fundamentalist religious beliefs were on trial in Dayton. When Darrow succeeded in getting Bryan himself on the witness stand, Bryan stated flatly that he believed that every word in the Bible was literally true. Darrow said to Bryan, you refuse "to choose between your crude, impossible beliefs and the common intelligence of modern times."

By now Scopes had been all but forgotten as the subject of the trial. Nevertheless, Bryan and the Dayton townspeople had their revenge against Darrow, and Scopes as well. The jury found Scopes guilty. But the judge fined him only $100.

Darrow appealed the case to the state supreme court. If necessary, he planned on appealing it to the U.S. Supreme Court, "Because," he said, "I think this case will be remembered as the first case of its kind since we stopped trying people in America for witchcraft."

However, the Tennessee Supreme Court later reversed the Scopes trial decision on a technicality, and the case never reached the U.S. Supreme Court.

Although the Scopes trial ended in what seemed to be an anticlimax, anti-evolution laws were seldom enforced after it was over. When an attempt was made to enforce them in the state of Arkansas, the U.S. Supreme Court promptly declared all such laws unconstitutional.

The Flag Salute Cases

The U.S. Supreme Court does not often dramatically reverse its own decisions. In the case of *Plessy v. Ferguson,* the Court ruled in favor of segregation. However, this opinion was reversed more than half a century later in the case of *Brown v. Board of Education.*

Another dramatic reversal occurred in what came to be called the Flag Salute Cases, which had to do with religious freedom. Fortunately, for the cause of civil liberty, the reversal did not take as long this time. Interestingly, the incidents involved in these cases took place during periods of national stress when the democratic processes of government were all too frequently ignored. That is, they occurred during a great economic depression and a major war.

The First Flag Salute Case

Mr. and Mrs. Walter Gobitis and their two children, Lillian, twelve, and William, ten, lived in the small town of Minersville, Pennsylvania. In the mid-1930s Minersville, like many other small towns in America, was in the grip of the Great Depression. However, money was not the major problem of the Gobitis family. Being allowed to practice their religion in freedom was.

The Gobitis family belonged to the Jehovah's Witnesses, an extremely strict religious faith. They believed strictly in God and His word as expressed in the Bible's Ten Commandments, especially the following three:

Thou shalt have no other gods before me.

Thou shalt not make unto thee any graven image, or any likeness of any thing that is in the heaven above, or that is in the earth beneath, or that is in the water under the earth.

Thou shalt not bow down thyself to them, nor serve them.

One day in 1936 young Lillian and William refused to join with the other public elementary school children in the daily classroom ritual of saluting the American flag and repeating the oath of allegiance. They refused to do so because it violated the Ten Commandments which said they should not bow down before a graven image. The Gobitis children were not being unpatriotic. It was simply that to them the American flag represented a graven image—something they were being forced to worship before God.

The principal of their grade school told Lillian and William they could no longer attend school if they refused to salute the American flag. The children returned home, told their parents about the incident, and their parents told them to continue to refuse to take part in the flag salute ritual.

A short time later the Minersville Board of Education met to discuss the problem. Its members decided that since the Gobitis children were not following the school rules, they should be expelled. Superintendent of Schools Charles E. Roudabush informed Mr. and Mrs. Walter Gobitis of the board's decision.

Walter Gobitis was a peace-loving man, but he was also a devout man and a father who dearly loved his children. Encouraged by the members of his church, he brought suit to prevent the Minersville Board of Education from making the flag salute a requirement for attending the local school. He did not object to the flag salute ritual; he simply objected to having his children forced to observe it. His suit also said that school attendance was compulsory in the state of Pennsylvania, but that his children were being kept out of the public schools by the Board of Education's ruling, and he could not afford to send his children to a private school.

The Federal District Court Judge in Philadelphia, Albert B. Maris, upheld Walter Gobitis' claim. The Minersville Board of Education then appealed the case to the U.S. Circuit Court of Appeals and finally to the Supreme Court when the circuit court upheld Judge Maris' decision.

By now it was 1939 and World War II had begun in Europe. America's entry into the war was being debated, and the fever of patriotism was running high. Public opinion—by now the Gobitis flag salute case was being widely discussed in the media—was strongly against anyone who refused to salute the American flag. The religious aspect of the case seldom was considered.

By now the Gobitis family also had much strong support on its side. Both the American Civil Liberties Union and the American Bar Association had seen their case as a flagrant attempt to violate the right of religious freedom of one unfortunate family. Lawyers from the Civil Liberties Union and the Bar Association presented powerful briefs. In part they said: "So far as the respondent children are concerned, the salute must be regarded as a religious ritual. We suggest that no American court should presume to tell any person that he is wrong in his opinion as to how he may best serve the God in which he believes.

"There is no such public need for the compulsory flag salute as to justify the overriding of the religious scruples of the children. Even if the challenged legislation be deemed to serve a public need, there are other reasonable ways of accomplishing the purpose without infringing the religious convictions of children."

In a direct reference to the war that was raging in Europe, the Gobitis briefs concluded: "The philosophy of free institutions is now being subjected to the most severe test it has ever undergone. Advocates of totalitarian government point to the speed and efficiency with which such systems are administered, and they assert that democracy can offer nothing to outweigh these advantages. The answer is to be found in the value of certain basic individual rights and the assurance afforded by free institutions that these shall not be required to yield to majority pressure no matter how overwhelming.

"The worth of our system must ultimately be judged in terms of the importance of those values and the care with which they are safeguarded. We consider them immeasurably important. We believe that the letter and spirit of our Constitution demand vindication of the individual liberties which are abridged by the challenged flag-salute regulation."

Despite this ardent plea, on June 3, 1940, the Supreme Court, in an eight to one decision, ruled against the Gobitis family. Reluctantly, the Court said, it agreed that the Minersville School Board had the authority to require a specified school program and that "the flag salute is an allowable portion of a school program."

Curiously, however, between the time when the Supreme Court had begun to hear the case and when it reached its final decision, public opinion had almost completely reversed itself. The eloquent briefs on behalf of the Gobitis family had not gone unheard throughout the nation, and the American people and the American press prided themselves in their basic beliefs in democracy. Perhaps someone's civil liberties *had* been violated. If so, the matter needed to be set right. Now only a few newspapers supported the Supreme Court decision. Almost two hundred of them were flatly opposed to it in their editorial columns.

Nevertheless, after the United States entered World War II and many members of Jehovah's Witnesses refused to serve in the military services on the grounds that they were conscientious objectors, much violence was used against them. Some of their meeting places were burned, many meetings were violently broken up, and in some states the Jehovah's Witnesses faith was outlawed. A number of children who continued to refuse to salute the American flag were sent to reformatories as juvenile delinquents. Consequently, it was not long before another Flag Salute Case arose for the Supreme Court's consideration. This time it occurred in West Virginia.

The Second Flag Salute Case

Based on the Supreme Court's decision in the Gobitis case, West Virginia's State Board of Education, in 1942, ordered school boards in all of the state's communities to "make the salute of the American flag a regular part of school program activities." Any refusal to salute the flag was to be regarded "as an act of insubordination and dealt with accordingly" by expulsion. Parents of expelled children were liable to be sent to jail.

Within a short time after this order was issued

104

many adult members of Jehovah's Witnesses and their children were being faced with prosecution for refusing to obey the order. Walter Barnette and several other parents applied together in the Charleston, West Virginia Federal District Court for an injunction against the enforcement of the state school board's order. Their request said that the order was unconstitutional because it was "a denial of religious freedom and free speech." By March 11, 1943, at the height of the war in Europe, the case of *West Virginia State Board of Education v. Barnette* reached the Supreme Court.

The Court handed down its decision on June 14, 1943, which was national Flag Day. By a vote of six to three the justices flatly reversed the earlier *Gobitis* decision. In reading the Court's majority opinion Justice and former United States Attorney General Robert H. Jackson said: "A person gets from a symbol the meaning he puts into it, and what is one man's comfort and inspiration is another's jest and scorn.

"To sustain the compulsory flag salute we are required to say that a Bill of Rights which guards the individual's right to speak his own mind, left it open to public authorities to compel him to utter what is not in his mind.

"Those who begin coercive elimination of dissent soon find themselves exterminating dissenters. Compulsory unification of opinion achieves only the unanimity of the graveyard. It seems trite but necessary to say that the First Amendment was designed to avoid these ends by avoiding these beginnings.

"If there is any fixed star in our constitutional constellation, it is that no official, high or petty, can prescribe what shall be orthodox in politics, nationalism, religion, or other matters of opinion or force citizens to confess by word or act their faith therein. If there are any circumstances which permit an exception, they do not now occur to us."

The Supreme Court's Continuing Role

Since the Flag Salute Cases the Supreme Court has had to rule on numerous other cases involving religion in the schools and its relationship to the Constitution's separation of church and state. Most of these cases have dealt with financial aid to parochial schools, Bible reading, and religious devotions such as prayers in public schools.

The Court has not been consistent in its decisions about parochial school aid. It decided partially in its favor (for bus transportation to and from school) in 1947 and partially against it (for transportation to and from field trips) in 1977. In 1975 the Court said that states could provide textbooks for secular private schools, but in 1977 it forbade state provision for instructional materials and equipment. Full federal financial aid for sectarian schools has not yet been finally ruled upon.

106

Bible Reading and Prayers in the Classroom

A national survey by the National Education Association taken in 1956 indicated that half of the states allowed the Bible to be read in the public schools. A later survey, taken in 1961, showed that one-third of the nation's school districts required classroom prayers. This was in spite of the fact that in 1948 the Supreme Court had ruled that a system of religious instruction in the Champaign, Illinois, public schools was unconstitutional. However, in 1962, the Supreme Court continued its efforts to keep religion out of the public school classroom when it ruled that the practice of public school prayer in New York State was clearly in violation of the First Amendment of the U.S. Constitution.

The Supreme Court's most recent rulings on separation of church and state have caused much public criticism and public comment about "Godlessness in the classroom." Several leading church figures and political spokesmen have proposed a constitutional amendment that would allow the right to religious devotion in all public schools. However, no such amendment has reached the floor of Congress. Neither Congress nor the Supreme Court, however, has heard the last of this question either in the schools or out of them.

The New Hampshire Flag Lowering Case

In the spring of 1978 New Hampshire Governor Meldrim Thomson, Jr., ordered the American flag lowered on all of his state's public buildings during Holy Week. He issued this order, Thomson said, to commemorate the death of Jesus Christ and as a sign of recognition that "the moral grandeur of Christianity is the bulwark against the forces of destructive ideologies."

However, five of the state's clergymen and the American Civil Liberties Union said Thomson's order was unconstitutional, and they sued to prevent the order from being carried out. United States District Judge Walter J. Skinner agreed that it was indeed unconstitutional, but the U.S. Court of Appeals upheld Thomson.

Consequently, on Good Friday morning all of New Hampshire's public flags were lowered to half-staff. Immediately the Civil Liberties Union appealed to the U.S. Supreme Court. The Court quickly ruled, five to four, that Thomson was acting in defiance of the U.S. Constitution's First Amendment. The New Hampshire governor obediently had the flags raised once more, but he promised that he would be back the following year with an order to lower the flags, not on religious but rather on secular grounds, to commemorate "the historical impact on Western civilization of the life and teachings of Jesus Christ."

There was little doubt that once again—as had happened so often in the past—the Supreme Court would have to face up to this challenge as well as numerous other challenges, both big and small, to the Constitution of the United States.

Thus, once again the Constitution, as interpreted by the Supreme Court, would prove to be a *living* Constitution—exactly as its authors intended it should be.

The Founding Fathers, of course, would undoubtedly be astonished at today's society that puts so many stresses and strains on the document they created. But they, like the Constitution, were flexible. They were the modern, up-to-date men of their day. They also had a firm and unswerving belief in American democracy. Consequently, they would undoubtedly be proud of the fact that their Constitution has completely become our Constitution and that it continues to live and serve democracy as well today as it did when it was written almost two centuries ago.

Bibliography

Allen, Frederick Lewis. *Only Yesterday, An Informal History of the 1920s.* New York: Harper & Row, 1931.
————. *Since Yesterday, 1929–1939.* New York: Harper & Row, 1940.
Coffey, Thomas M. *The Long Thirst, Prohibition in America: 1920–1933.* New York: Dell Publishing Co., 1976.
Garraty, John A. *Quarrels That Have Shaped the Constitution.* New York: Harper & Row, 1975.
Kelly, Alfred H. and Harbison, Winifred A. *The American Constitution, Its Origins and Development.* New York: W. W. Norton, 1963.
McCloskey, Robert Green. *The Modern Supreme Court.* Cambridge: Harvard University Press, 1972.
Morison, Samuel Eliot. *The Oxford History of the American People.* New York: Oxford University Press, 1965.
Salomon, Leon I. *The Supreme Court.* Vol. 33, *The Reference Shelf,* New York: H. W. Wilson, 1961.
Schwartz, Bernard. *A Basic History of the Supreme Court.* Princeton: Van Nostrand, 1968.

111

————. *The Law in America*. New York: American Heritage Publishing Co., 1974.

Stevens, Leonard. *Equal: The Case of Integration vs. Jim Crow*. New York: Coward, McCann & Geoghegan, 1975.

————. *Salute: The Case of the Bible Versus the Flag*. New York: Coward, McCann & Geoghegan, 1973.

————. *Trespass: The People's Privacy vs. Power of the Police*. New York: Coward, McCann & Geoghegan, 1977.

Warren, Charles. *The Supreme Court in United States History*. Boston: Little, Brown, 1922.

Index

115

INDEX

117

About the Author

Don Lawson's interest in history has led him to write more than twenty books for young people, including *The Secret World War II, Democracy* (A First Book) and *Morocco, Algeria, Tunisia, and Libya* (A First Book) for Franklin Watts. His interest in education is reflected in his authorship of *Education Careers*, also for Franklin Watts, and in his position as editor in chief of United Educators—publishers of *American Educator Encyclopedia*. Mr. Lawson and his wife, Bea, live in Chicago, Illinois.